HOW TO BE SUCCESSFUL IN SALES

BY RON GIORDANO

HOW TO BE SUCCESSFUL IN SALES
by RON GIORDANO

ISBN: 978-1-59298-736-8

Library of Congress Catalog Number: 2017909538

Book design and typesetting: Rick Korab, Punch Design, Inc.
Printed in the United States of America

First Printing: May 2017

21 20 19 18 17   5 4 3 2 1

BEAVER'S POND
PRESS

Beaver's Pond Press, Inc.
7108 Ohms Lane
Edina, MN 55439–2129

(952) 829-8818
www.BeaversPondPress.com

To order, visit www.ItascaBooks.com or call 1-800-901-3480 ext. 118.
Reseller discounts available.

ACKNOWLEDGEMENTS

There are are hundreds of people who contributed to the creation of this book in one way or another that I would like to thank. First and foremost, , I want to thank my parents, Nick and Florence, who gave me the direction I needed to succeed in any endeavor thought possible. They taught me that all you need is to believe in yourself—and never forget the people who have helped you along the way. My mother was always there for me and Dad made me feel like a king.

My wife, Darla, through her everlasting understanding and support has allowed me, not only to succeed but to thrive. She is my lover, my best friend, my shoulder to rest on. I realize I've been something of a challenge, but she has always been on my side. I never had to spend a moment worrying about my family because I know what a capable, smart and loving woman she is. Darla is my rock. My wonderful children never complained about the fact that I was away so often. My son Ron and daughter Courtney were and continue to be a blessing for my wife and I. They each have identities that personify the love we have for both of them. I would give my life for my children.

There are people I have met along the way who have had a particular effect on me and when I look back, I realize what a lucky man I am. Al Trice, who gave me an opportunity by hiring me, and then had enough confidence to turn me loose to do my own thing, has my undying gratitude. Thank you so much, my good friend. To Richard Kauffman who believed in me enough to allow me to be the "entrepreneur" in sales and gave me the reins of the company, recognizing my dedication to the job's responsibilities and my loyalty to the company. To the nuns at the St. Vincent's orphanage, to Leo, to Ms. Ruth Van Sickle Ford, and to my in-laws, relatives and friends. To the co-workers and friends I have lost: you climbed the mountain and your journey has ended, but not without leaving a memory forever in my mind and my soul. I always have been able to find a helping hand extended along the way and I hope to do the same for others whenever and however I can. Thanks to each and every one of you, including Mike Bozzini, who referred to me as the voice.

When this book began it was merely a thought in the back of my mind. As I began to write some thoughts down, it seemed as though it might actually evolve into something more than I had anticipated. At that point, I knew that I needed someone to give me direction, edit my work, and to offer suggestions. I was very lucky to find an editor in San Francisco with whom I made a wonderful connection. I hope we'll be lifelong friends and collaborators. Patricia Hernandez acted as a mentor and shared her knowledge of the mechanics of writing a book. I cannot thank her enough.

DEDICATION

There are loved ones, friends, and co-workers that could be recognized in this dedication, but I have instead chosen to dedicate this book to the children of the world, particularly to those who are ill, in need of love and care, and to those who will never have the opportunity to live the kind of happy life I have had the fortune to enjoy. We all have our ups and downs—times when we are unhappy with our lives— but eventually, often with some help, we get through it. Children are our lifeline to the future, and for those kids who are in need, we must step up and recognize that they are not always able to help themselves.

All profits from this book will be directed to children, especially those who are ill and may never see tomorrow. We can, at the very least, try to create some joy for them; we can let them know we really do care. The profits from this book are only a drop in the bucket, but it's some-thing,. It's a beginning, and it feels so darn good to share.

TABLE OF CONTENTS

PREFACE

. . . .

Most people are born with gifts they never even realize they have. What happens? They miss the chance to take advantage of what nature has so generously given them, simply because they aren't paying attention. They miss a lot of "could have beens," and I think that's something of a heartbreak. A wise man once said "The saddest thing in life is wasted talent." Gifts and talents aren't necessarily limited to having the voice of a songbird or playing the violin like a virtuoso; they are often seemingly simple things: a dynamite smile that radiates in a crowd, the ability to throw a wicked curveball. It can also be an uncanny and profound ability to feel what others are feeling, a sense of empathy, or the ability to comfort someone just the right way. Of course many of us have gifts everyone is aware of, mostly because we've told them so. This book is about identifying and honing your talents so you can find success, not only in sales, but in all your endeavors both professional and personal.

Part of my success has been my ability to understand and analyze others. I call it "reading" someone. I believe this is one of my gifts. My wife has often stated that, "your eyes are the window to your soul," and I believe this wholeheartedly. In a nutshell, I believe that whatever your background and situation, you can fashion yourself a successful and happy life by learning to maintain a positive attitude, following your instincts, and communicating effectively. We are all God's children, and though we may not see things the same way others do, we all need to find compassion and common ground whenever we can, particularly in business. I learned a lot from my parents and family members when I was growing up and I use those lessons every day—they become habit after a while. If you can't draw upon your own family's wisdom for some reason, you must find inspiration and support elsewhere. This really isn't as difficult as one might imagine when you always have your eyes (and ears) open. With confidence, finding a support system of friends and acquaintances isn't so very hard. This world offers so much. If you say you have no friends, doesn't that really mean you're not seeking them? I understand that many people are shy. I hope my advice will be helpful to the "wallflowers" out there. It is possible to find loved ones, even if you aren't related. I have discovered throughout my life what should be common sense: people who share easily are usually good-hearted people. If you want to meet your town or city's most honest and good-hearted people, spend a Thanksgiving serving food to the poor. I promise you'll have a smile on your face all day and for weeks to follow, along with new friends if you're willing to put yourself out there.

My father always made it a priority to be charitable. He was generous to a fault. When I reached a certain point in life, I decided the best way I could help others was not merely through financial means or by speaking to my employees, clients, or children —but by writing this book. While it is aimed mostly at folks in the sales field, the advice I have to offer can be applied on a much wider scale. While I can give you tips on how to close a deal or how not to freeze when making cold calls, my advice can be germane to a number of fields including your home life and family. Call it a "Sales Book Plus" if you will. Since the beginning of time, people have interpreted and recorded life through cave drawings and great pieces of literature to stories told around a desert campfire to impart wisdom, to describe history, and to amuse. I write this book mainly to help and to remind you, the reader, of what you can do if you only give it your best try…if you never give up.

Helping, to me, means understanding without taking sides. Many times, in both your personal and business life, you'll find that you can avoid the position as aggravator in lieu of that of a mediator. The key is to rest on logic and reason, allowing you to make the best judgment calls. In any field, you'll do well to embrace patience and understanding. Clients or potential clients, will be most grateful, as will any staff you work with. So often, people you work with don't do what you expect of them. Does that mean you should rave like a maniac? Does scaring or intimidating people work for you? It is so much more efficient (and so much more human) to take a step back and rethink your stance. Remember, the scowling gentleman across the desk from you is not your family pet or your naughty three-year-old. Even if a client is near impossible to deal with, your best move is to kill them with kindness. Force your smile to grow, make a joke if it's appropriate, try to get the conversation back on a neutral track and find common ground. This takes practice, but once you master the skill of defusing potential bombs, you'll know to use that skill in every aspect of your life. There's a tool for you: always kill them with kindness.

We have all experienced the dynamics of relationships, from the families we are born into to the families we make; from the friends we surround ourselves with to our work colleagues; from our neighbors to the community at large. I have been fortunate—my parents, my wife, and my best friends have all allowed me to be steady, caring, and understanding, because they offer the same to me. In fact, they have encouraged it. When it comes to the other folks who walk in and out of my life, mainly people in the workplace, I have learned how to play nicely in the sandbox. Adults can often let their inner three-year-old out, and it isn't pretty. I'll show you in Chapter Eight how to cope with some of the personalities you're bound to run across.

I cannot claim that this book is the equivalent of a Harvard Business School education, but based on my years in the business and my insatiable curiosity about how it all works, I have written this book based upon actual events and opportunities that I created for myself. If there's one positive I learned forgoing a college education, it is that it is necessary to set rules and goals for yourself. It's something like learning to swim by being thrown into the deep end of the pool. It can be scary at first, but the rewards are great. After struggling a bit, you learn to think for yourself. You create your own ideas, and you begin to "think outside the box" for a lack of textbooks and busy professors. I succeeded through hard work, but I want to make it easier for you: I want to teach you to motivate yourself. I am sure that you have heard that before, probably from your mom and dad, a friend in school, or your boss. So who am I to tell you?

I'm a regular guy from an old Chicago Italian neighborhood. I'm a guy who likes to do nice things when I can, even if it's for the selfish prize of seeing someone smile. I'm a guy who was drawn to drawing and who was lucky enough to attend the Chicago Academy of Fine Art, but who had to have the Dean assist me with my word pronunciation because my T's all sounded like D's. I'm a guy who started at the very bottom and worked my way up without stepping on others. I'm a guy who respected what his dad taught him: a handshake is a contract, and so are the promises you make to others. My success did not come merely because I'm a "good guy"; it came because I made it a priority in my life to be successful without ever considering failure as an option. If you do the job right, with honesty and integrity, success will follow. That is what I firmly believe. What I share with you in this book is how I succeeded and, moreover, how you can do it as well.

We are all different, but we all share common threads. We all want success of one kind or another, whether it's in raising children, coming in below par, or having the greenest lawn on the block. The story in this book is as basic as it gets, but sometimes when we clear away all the clutter and get down to the bare basics, we're able to see more clearly. We're more able to understand the simple fundamentals that make someone successful. I don't particularly want to instruct you to do it my way; you won't find pie charts, exercises, or statistical graphs here. Instead, I hope to teach by example. The man- ner in which I applied myself in certain scenarios may give you some ideas as to how you can use your own unique style and approach to reach your goals. Everybody is different, but everybody has a chance— that's what I want to drive home. The greatest thing in the world is to be able to help others. Some do it with money and awards; I like to do it with thoughts, ideas, and examples so that you can spread your wings and soar into the entrepreneurial world without ever having to dive-bomb anyone in your way. What is most important in the end, whether in sales or any other profession, is how you feel about yourself and the job you've done. Happy work lives make for happy personal lives and happy family lives. That's what we're all really after, isn't it?

I also hope to bring a smile to your face from time to time. For me, that's pure magic. There is not a salesperson alive who doesn't have an amazing, mind-bending, knee-slapping story or twelve to tell. A book about sales needn't be dry or stuffy. No one ever said that learning couldn't be done while laughing. My greatest wish is to excite you, to motivate you, to see the silver lining in every situation. This truly is an "outside of the box" project for me. I've certainly learned a lot during this book's creation, and I hope you'll enjoy this little gift of wisdom from a guy who followed his gut instinct, who found a thoroughly satisfying life, and thought he'd share just how it happened.

PART ONE

· · · · · · · · · · · · · · · ·

The Roots Nourish the Blossom

CHAPTER ONE

. . . .

"Dis" and "Dat"

When I was growing up in Chicago on the near West Side—a neighborhood filled with a mix of Italian, Black, and Greek families—my dad
worked six and a half days a week as the manager of a Ford dealership.
When the state of Illinois passed legislation preventing car dealerships from running their crews ragged, the dealerships simply closed
on Sundays, since the owners wouldn't think of working on Sundays
themselves. My father was different, though. He was never
concerned about his days off because providing for his family took
precedence over actually spending time with us. He didn't come to
ballgames or play with us, but he was at home every evening. My father was old-fashioned that way and was the model of dependability.

My older brother and I were very often surrounded by our large
Italian family. Aunts, uncles, and cousins were so numerous that during
holiday celebrations we needed three different rooms for everyone
to dine. In the back bedroom, my aunts would place huge bins of
marvelous ravioli covered with flour to keep them moist before
cooking. The teenagers ate in the small living room, the main dining
room was for the adults, and the kitchen was where the small children
(and sometimes a drunken uncle) were relegated.

After three main courses, it was traditionally time to play cards. The
adults took over the living room and enjoyed their card games into
the wee hours of the night, pausing only to get up and choose from
a cornucopia of desserts. In the kitchen, a grand gathering of ladies
gossiped and chatted whilst washing, drying, and putting seemingly
countless dishes away. We kids just laughed and chased and caroused
wherever there was open space. It was a controlled chaos of almost
tangible love and respect. Brilliant in their energy, these were my favorite days of the year. I knew people loved me and cared about me.

More importantly, I saw how they treated each other with respect, kindness, and generosity. That supportive environment absolutely shaped my decisions and notions as I grew into a man, both with family and with career. I always felt that if we simply took care of and supported each other that the outcome would always turn out well. This has been true in both my personal and professional life.

I'm certainly aware that many children lack the luxury of a strong and supportive family life. This doesn't prevent them from surrounding themselves with people who take their responsibilities as a human being seriously. They provide honesty, sympathy, and a willingness to better society no matter their given circumstance. It's not an issue of class, race, religion, or anything else. I knew kids whose parents were in a constant state of battle; I saw women with black eyes. I knew early on that I was fortunate when God assigned babies to families; I also knew some folks who were very unfortunate and it broke my heart.

That said, I'm proud of the fact that I grew up in a fairly rough-and-tumble neighborhood. I attended grade school at Resurrection on the West Side, where I was also an altar boy. I was the short, quiet kid in grade school, but I immediately joined the local neighborhood gang called the Junior Lords when I was a pre-teen. In my neighborhood, if you didn't join you didn't belong. We were too young to get involved in street fights and such, but back then, shootings were certainly a rarity and drugs were pretty much limited to stealing one of Dad's beers. We tried to mimic the older Lords and they were charitable enough to play baseball with us on occasion. We played this favorite pastime of ours often, competing with other teams in the Chicago Park District League. Once a year, though, we would play the "big game" against the Senior Lords. We almost always lost, but the game always boasted a sell-out crowd under the lights at Clark's Field. It was true Chicago style softball, using a 16" Clincher (a Chicago staple and the only city where it is used). For us, this was as good as it got. The rest of the time, we just stood around with slicked-backed hair, trying to look menacing. Why? We are all human and we were in that phase of young manhood. We caused a bit of trouble, but for the most part my folks never found out.

During those years I didn't have much in the way of material goods, but I had dreams. When I was in grade school, I built a hot dog stand in the basement of our apartment house. It was just an old, dark, musty space with a coal furnace, but I didn't care. Even then, I had the heart of a businessman. I was born an entrepreneur, though I didn't know it until I was much older.

Ironically, and perhaps as a portent of things to come, I never did sell a single hot dog because as soon as I finished the construction of the stand, a friend stopped by and liked it so much he bought it. It was my first real sale, but I didn't stop there. I had new projects to move on to, including helping neighbors with work around their houses. One gentleman needed help with tuckpointing on his building. He showed me what to do, I picked up the technique quickly, and soon I was enjoying the jingle of coins in my pocket. My parents thought that I was too young to be working, but always adept at the art of convincing they gave me the go-ahead to experiment with my newfound sales techniques. Although he wasn't an effusive man I knew my father was impressed.

My parents bought their first home when I was a teenager. I was still short and quiet when I entered St. Philip's High School, but when I started my senior year I finally began to grow. What a relief. Coming from my neighborhood, and then moving further into the heart of that community, meant a necessary continued allegiance to the Junior Lords. Older now, we were destined for more serious trouble. What we referred to as "gang life" involved defending ourselves fairly often. Yes, on occasion I fought just for the hell of it. Along the way though, I developed some profound friendships that last through today. We depended on each other; we laughed together and we cried together. There was a real camaraderie but it was quite different than the bond I had with my family. Both included loyalty, responsibility, honesty, and always lending a hand when needed. This is taken to a fault today with gangs. Instead of fists and fat lips, it's guns and decimated bodies.

Back in my day, the gang life actually had some positive influence on me. I saw how group dynamics function and further honed my ability to read people, something that would serve me well over and over in the future. I noticed that by keeping quiet and looking at someone carefully, I could "read" them. In other words, I could tell a lot about someone by observing their eyes, their movements, their gestures and stance. It wasn't such a big deal at the time (except when my instinct told me to run), but I appreciated this gift which often resulted in a favorable outcome for me. People opened up to me easily.

Naturally, when I reached a certain age, I needed to decide what to do with myself. I followed my heart into art—certainly a visual field—with a lot of help from family and friends. An older acquaintance of mine spoke to me one day about attending the Chicago Academy of Fine Art and enrolling in a graphic arts program. I guess my love for art began when I was a boy. I liked to participate in the ads in magazines that offered to assess your drawing skills if you copied the picture they provided and sent it in. Apparently I had some real talent, at least according to the magazine folks. The "contests" turned out to be ads for an art school, so not much came of that, but it did give me the encouragement to keep practicing. I spent many hours sketching and designing logos as well as creating ideas for magazine ads.

I also enjoyed taking snapshots with a camera a thoughtful relative had given me, designing each shot for composition and visual appeal. My parents, had always encouraged me to paint and draw and express my creativity—I was so lucky in that respect. They never saw it as a waste of time; they took joy in my enthusiasm.

Each morning I had class, I'd take the L train or I'd get a lift from my brother to school in downtown Chicago, then walk the rest of the way with my bag stuffed full of art supplies. My experience at the Academy was invaluable. Though I didn't wind up working as a commercial artist for a long period of time, the Institute taught me about my abilities, my opportunities, and how I could make things happen simply by working hard and never quitting or giving up, no matter how frustrated I was. In classes like painting, design, anatomy, perspective, and creative design, my ability to think outside the box blossomed. The ability to communicate through pen and paper or watercolor on canvas helped me tremendously with interacting with others. In order to get my message across, I had to see through my viewers' eyes. Who would have thought that a degree in art would help me so much in a sales career?

The dining table at home was the only place with enough space for me to work, so that became my home, often into the early hours of the morning. On many a late night (or early morning), my mother would wake me and remind me to go to bed because when I was painting, the time just seemed to roll right by. Leo, who happened to be the general manager of a sign company, invited me to use the drawing boards at his office, then purchased a drawing board for me, which I still have today. Over the coming months, my benefactor Leo was always willing to provide me with whatever I needed so long as I worked hard and stayed in school. I'm still amazed by his generosity. How did I draw such kindness and generosity? I know now, but I didn't know then. It is the very same set of principles I'll be sharing in the pages to follow. I know that I never took any of these favors for granted; instead, I promised myself that I would always help other people. Some folks call it karma; I call it a way of life.

I was thrilled to be in this new environment—surrounded by academics, but with a focus on the creative. There were rules and theories I sometimes disagreed with, but I disagreed with excitement, not anger. I was hungry at the Academy and my enthusiasm and excitement parlayed into success—another lesson well worth learning. I found that when I was genuinely excited about something, success was almost a given. At one point, I decided to branch out into new territory and entered a design contest for the House of Vision, a popular eyewear company in Chicago. Though I'd certainly never done anything like it before, I worked on a unique pair of frames and won third place. It was a triumph! Not only had I succeeded, I had done so outside of my comfort zone. Now I knew for sure that the world could, in fact, be my oyster. The support I had been lucky enough to receive throughout my life—from a number of different sources—had given me a very special advantage: I had confidence. I believed in myself and I had learned to trust my intuition.

My years at the Academy also expanded my horizons with regard to social interaction. I was in a very different part of the City, studying alongside a very different group of people than, say, the Junior Lords, who I had left behind save a few lifelong pals. To my surprise, however, I found I could communicate with just about anyone effectively. I could be a chameleon, but I was very aware of how my voice and mannerisms changed; I didn't want to come across as dishonest or false. But while I was particularly good at dealing with clients and such, I had a problem that just couldn't be ignored.

The Dean of the Academy at that time was Ruth Van Sickle Ford, a very well-respected watercolor artist. One day she called me into her office. "Ron," she said, "I'm going to tell you something that might hurt your feelings, but it really is for your own good." I waited with anxiety to hear her criticism. "Ron," she continued, "your grammar and pronunciation are atrocious." I was about to learn another lesson that would change the course of my future. If I wanted to make something of myself, I had to speak English, and if I was going to learn to speak properly, I was going to speak as elegantly and clearly as a Harvard grad.

I regarded Ruth with great respect, so each day after class, I'd go to her office and practice, which consisted mainly of learning the difference between T's and D's—after all, it was the way everyone in my neighborhood spoke. Ruth was an angel for caring enough to spend that extra time helping me out. I was embarrassed at first, but she was kind and patient and by the end of the year, my speech was the very definition of articulate. "Do unto others…" I reminded myself often.

With my "dis" and "dat" fully under control, I began to experiment with tone and speech patterns, along with developing a more impressive vocabulary. Obviously, speaking clearly and professionally is a must for anyone working with the public. I still give Ms. Van Sickle all the credit when a client asks me what college I attended. I wasn't aware of it then, but Ruth's lessons would be yet another key to my future success. My family and friends back in the neighborhood teased me, asking time after time if I'd do the "newscaster" voice. After a while, this "tool" became second nature; when I opened my mouth to speak, the words just flowed. I'm convinced that the majority of my sales deals would have failed without the help of that dear woman. The lessons—or tools—I needed to achieve my goals were adding up.

With the limited free time I had, I decided to help out at St. Vincent's orphanage. In past years, I had phoned the Mother Superior and offered to entertain the kids on Easter. A friend and I had dressed up in Easter Rabbit costumes and handed out candy. Is it odd that a teenage boy would offer up a Sunday they could otherwise spend playing street hockey or hanging out at the park? I didn't find it so then. I always liked children—especially happy ones. Coming across a child who was crying or in some distress had always gotten me all choked up. These kids were orphans, something which particularly saddened me as I had such a wonderful family, and I wanted to see if I could make them laugh—inject a little fun into their lives. My own home life was so nurturing and full of love and laughter; I figured I'd pass some along.

My family loved children, too, and I often took the kids to my parents' home or to the park nearby, accompanied by several nurses. On our first visit to Mom and Dad's place, something miraculous happened. As we entered the back yard, I heard gasps from the kids and I watched as, en masse, they all ran to my mother's flowerbed. In their few years on the planet, they'd never seen a living flower until then; they'd grown up surrounded by concrete. Who knew something so simple could be so well appreciated?

While at the Academy, days spent at the orphanage were even more poignant, sometimes gut-wrenching, simply because I was a man now and I knew more of the realities of life. What could I give them to make them feel a little better? What could I offer? The answer was easy. The orphanage building was five stories tall, with the fourth floor devoted to the oldest children who ranged in age from three to five years old. The Mother Superior laughed like a kid herself when I asked if I could add some colorful decoration to the dormitory hallways. It was probably the hardest I'd ever worked on a project because so much love was put into it. Soon Mickey Mouse, Pluto, Peter Pan, and an array of other characters danced across the walls. In the nursery school classroom, where flaking, drab mint green paint had been the décor, a jungle took over—lions, tigers, and monkeys frolicking everywhere.

On something of an artistic spree, I went on to paint all of the equipment in St. Vincent's confined concrete play area. We were in the heart of the city and there wasn't much of a yard, so I decorated any surface I could find with brightness, something to bring a smile. I had the biggest smile of anyone on earth the first time the kids saw what I'd done. Random acts of kindness are underappreciated and have fallen into disuse, I'm afraid. But think what the benefits are. The cosmos has a very interesting method of directing good energy. No, I'm not one of those New Age types—I just know that doing good brings its just rewards.

When I finished at the Art Academy, I had to say goodbye to the Mother Superior, the nuns, and the children at the orphanage. I had decided to join the Army. In 1960, with the Cold War in full swing and Cuba posing a threat, it was either join or get drafted. I thought that by volunteering, I had a better chance of landing a position that would fit my background in art or graphics, something away from any battlefields, anyway. Maybe by joining I could even get out faster and continue what I thought would be a promising career in graphic arts.

After my basic training at Ft. Leonard Wood, Missouri, I was transferred to Ft. Gordon, Georgia for training at the Military Police (MP) school. When I had a free moment I would go out into the backwoods of Georgia and paint the abandoned gin mills using watercolors on blotter board. I couldn't just blot out the artist in me. I needed it to express myself in what were less than ideal conditions. Because I had listed my profession as "artist," the Army made me an MP. I don't understand the logic either.

During the day, I'd patrol with my partner in either Augusta or Savannah, which was part of regular training after finishing MP school. In essence, we were "on the job" police officers without a hell of a lot of experience. The idea, though, was to keep the soldiers fresh and ready at all times. At night I'd revert back to my role as the humble artist. When the generals in Washington began to feel itchy about the Dominican Republic, my partner and I were chosen for several special assignments. I fully understood how terrifying it could be for those caught up in an uprising.

One night when we got back to camp, my heart almost burst from my chest when I was told I'd received mail from home. The fellow handed me a box with a return address from the orphanage. I sat on my cot and sorted through photos, drawings, and letters from the kids, and a personal note from the Mother Superior herself. I continue to hold those items dear to my heart and close at hand. When I need inspiration or comfort, I return to them and I feel the same spark I did when I first received them. It was a treasure of a gift that keeps on giving...and none of it had cost a cent.

CHAPTER TWO

. . . .

This and That

When I finished my six-month tour, I still had five-and-a-half years of reserve duty left, but the first thing I really needed was a job. I knew exactly what I wanted to do: graphic arts for a large and busy organization. The thing was, I wasn't very patient when it came to my career. I didn't want to be a runner, which is how most folks start out; I wanted to be on the drawing board right away. I searched far and wide until I found an opening at the Columbia Envelope Co., and it's there that I would begin my career as an artist on the drawing board. "Perseverance," I shouted out to myself while shaving on the morning of my first day at work. "If you really, really want it, you have to persevere until your dream is reality." My pick of "tools" was getting larger, but objectively speaking, I was still pretty green.

I left Columbia in 1965 to go to work for the Hélène Curtis Co. It was a natural step up for me and a new environment, full of new faces, including the gorgeous face of my soon-to-be wife, Darla, named after the most adorable member of the "Spanky and Our Gang" kids. (I suppose that would make me Alfalfa.) I was in the art department and she was employed in the beauty supply division, after transferring over from the consumer division. Intelligent, caring, industrious, lovely to look at, and delightful to see, how lucky could I get? From the moment I saw her, I hoped she'd be my wife.

Not too long after I met Darla, I became acquainted with the owner of a lounge where my buddies and I spent time. One night he asked me, "Ron, listen, there's a beauty salon—a place my wife goes to. Anyway, it's for sale and I have half a mind to buy the place. What do you think? Are you interested in being half owner?" I really wasn't interested in the beauty business, but the entrepreneur in me would have nothing to do with mulling it over. I just wanted to be in business whatever that business was. I yearned for the challenge I was missing out on at the old nine-to-fiver. Plus, I was already working for Helene Curtis, one of the biggest beauty enterprises in the world. It took less than five minutes for me to answer, "Why not!" After all, nothing ventured nothing gained. We each pitched in the grand sum of $500 and bought the business, which was a little more run-down than we'd been led to believe.

My life was very full, and a year later, the shop was in the same sorry condition. We were barely breaking even. I'd done what my grand-mother used to say at the dessert table at holiday time. "Ron, watch out, your eyes are bigger than your stomach." I'd thought that working full time and running a small business would be a cinch. I was wrong. Here comes another lesson: you need people to support and help you, no matter what. The truth was, my partner was busy with his lounge and didn't want to spend any time or money on the salon. He looked at it as a tax write-off where I looked at it as an opportunity. I decided that the only way to turn the place into a profit-maker was to take it over myself. I bought my partner out for $600 and I gave the place a complete overhaul.

We all have our own unique character traits—one of mine is an almost obsessive need to succeed, and I was determined to turn this challenge into a success come hell or high water. I wanted—I demanded—add-ed value down the road. I couldn't run the shop on a day to day basis, but I could find people who I trusted—and who trusted me—to help out. I began recruiting friends and family members who were not only willing and able to lend a hand, most were very experienced hands. My aunt, for example, was a hairstylist and my mother managed operations and scheduled appointments with finesse. They were tickled to pitch in—they were excited to be a part of a new enterprise and they sure didn't mind the extra income.

I learned quickly that finding and hiring the right people to surround yourself with is every bit as important as any other aspect of a business. The right people don't just stop by, poke their head in, and ask, "Hey, you look like you need help!" Slowly but surely, and through much trial and error, I learned to open the lines of communication with my customers, my vendors, and my stylists, letting them know exactly what I was looking for. I dropped in at the local beauty schools and let them know I needed top-notch graduating students, even offering incentives to the schools—the old "you scratch my back and I'll scratch yours." I encouraged my stylists to enter styling contests, paying the entry fee so that they could, in turn, promote the shop. I learned the art of networking during this period of my career. Add another tool to the list.

While I was developing my staff, I also needed to improve the salon's look. With my arts education, I should have realized earlier just how important appearances are. Luckily, my soon to be father-in-law, Lou, was kind enough, and saw enough promise in me, to help out with the remodeling of the salon. Lou and I got along great—he was a whiz of a carpenter and we worked together terrifically as long as I followed his lead and learned from his experience, then demonstrated what I could do and how well I could do it. He respected sincerity and honesty and I respected his ability to guide me in a direct way, showing me the shortcuts that come with being an experienced craftsman. We spent many hours together and we had an understanding that I was the apprentice and he was the journeyman, although he always treated me as an equal. I learned that as long as I could accept my role, understanding that others may know more than I did, I never resented instruction or suggestions from him, even if they were barked rather than peppered with pleases and thank-you's. I recognized then that I could give up my pride for something much more valuable: knowledge.

A buddy of mine installed some new plumbing. I put up some nice wallpaper, painted, and added more sinks in an unused area in the back. I landscaped and spruced up the front window area and installed a new sign: Ron's Beauty Garden Salon. Voilà! Now I had an establishment I could really be proud of, being operated by people I loved and trusted.

Next, I dove into promotion and marketing on a scale I was capable of handling. Special offers were advertised on permanents, cuts, and colors, and I even made a deal with Hélène Curtis to handle their hair-piece line. I was delighted when Hélène Curtis introduced a new line of ladies' hair pieces—I had an "in" there. I made an appointment with the HC marketing department and asked the VP there all about the new line. It hadn't been out long, and I learned that what they needed most at that point was some exposure. A bit nervously, I admitted that I owned a beauty salon on the side and I wanted to exhibit their product. Some eyebrows rose at first, but by the time I was done selling the idea, everyone agreed it would be a sensational idea to install a booth in my salon. I would buy the hair pieces at a wholesale cost and mark them up to sell, and the booth would remain free of charge as long as I highlighted and pushed their product. I always say, "nothing ventured, nothing gained." If I hadn't made that walk over to the marketing department that day, I would have missed out on a sterling opportunity. My toolbox was beginning to fill up and with it, so was my confidence and my ability to keep thinking of new and innovative ways of molding a very satisfying career for myself.

In the four years I kept Ron's Beauty Garden Salon, I got a crash course in operations across the board. I performed all the financial tasks with the help of my mother, who as my dad would say, really needed something to occupy her time since my brother had moved out and Dad was still working full time. Her aid was invaluable, especially on the busiest days—Thursday through Saturday. During the first year, we employed three stylists on a semi-regular basis and served perhaps twenty customers per day. After the second year, and particularly after the remodel, we had five stylists, a shampoo girl, and a manicurist. Over the holidays that year, we served an average of one hundred and five customers a day. "I can do this," I thought to myself. "And if I can do this, I can do anything!"

That got me to thinking. I've never been one to remain stagnant for long, so after nearly five years at the salon, I decided to put the ship up for sale to see if perhaps I could build myself a yacht. My confidence was about to take me into uncharted waters, but my nerves were steady. I had the gift of confidence. It had been a terrific run, but I was forever expanding my life plan and I knew that my next intended step would take still more of my time. I knew that it was better to sell on the top end and move on—the sale would generate enough cash to put a down payment on a home for Darla and I and what we hoped would be a growing family.

I remember sitting on the salon steps with Darla on the day the sale went through. We laughed ourselves silly when I finally admitted to her that I'd always been a little bit shy about telling people I owned a beauty salon. Some of the comments I received (which I will not be sharing with you) shall stay buried in my mind's vault for all of eternity. It wasn't the kind of business venture I had envisioned going into at any part of my life, but it had been an opportunity to make something out of nothing and we were both very proud.

I had done relatively well for myself. My initial investment of $1,100 (plus the money I'd spent on the remodel) turned into an impressive profit—I sold The Beauty Garden for $10,000. Add that to the daily profit I'd enjoyed as the owner and I felt very pleased indeed with my blossoming business acumen. Did I know what I was doing? Not really, but I had the confidence to move forward simply because I felt in my gut that I could do it. I was determined to continue rising up the free market ladder—rung by rung, if necessary. If I felt the need to trust my gut over what was deemed "common sense" or "the way everyone else did it," so be it. I'd always been an entrepreneur, after all, and the "no risk, no gain" idea really drove me. How many chances do you have if you don't take advantage of situations that present themselves? If I hadn't followed my nose and instinct, I never would have gotten to where I am today. Once I got into the field, it was a whole new world—one in which there were no boundaries, only the sky to reach for.

When you rely upon your instinct instead of following someone else's steps to success, it almost always works out for the better. If, by chance, it isn't, don't hang your head and lose your spark—keep moving forward! You've got to put one foot forward first before another can respond to your ideas or efforts. Venturing outside of the box can consist of anything from a new product idea or a new concept in ordering, a new package design or a unique way of marketing. Never sell yourself short by not venturing out in the world; get out of the cold and move into the warmth of creativity. That's what keeps you alive and kicking in business. I still had no idea where life would eventually take me all I knew was that whatever I was doing was working, so that seemed to be the best path to follow—using my instinct as a guide.

I'd always gotten along so well with people; I recall a client once commenting that I could sell an egg to a chicken. Working in the art department at Hélène Curtis was rewarding in many ways, but I craved more contact with people in general rather than being cooped up in an office all day long. I'd always preferred working in the field, so when I left Curtis to work for an ad agency in 1966, it was only meant to be a temporary move. I would marry Darla the following year. The advertising business really appealed to me and, as before, I wanted to get to work on the drawing board right away. I didn't want to start out as a "runner." My vast reserves of energy and drive came from my overwhelming sense of responsibility, initially to my parents, then to my wife, but also because I truly desired success. Why else were we here on earth if not to interact, to introduce new things to a new audience, to express creativity and innovation? I put my nose to the grindstone and stopped at nothing. I relied upon my work ethic and my personality and graphic design ability to help my customers, never losing my focus. My success resulted from dedication, determination, and desire.

I ended up staying at the ad agency for a little more than a year, but it just wasn't an environment I was happy working in. I was, in fact, frustrated, again, finding myself indoors all day with no direct, daily contact with clients. Since my initial objective had been to work with people, I knew it was time to make another change. I knew my ship would come in eventually if I didn't allow myself to see it slip. I had to remain patient, observant, and no matter how frustrating things could become, I had to keep a steel grip on my confidence, both in myself and in the world.

My next move was to a direct mail printing company in downtown Chicago, where I worked for about two years. I had already begun looking for something else before long, though, because I could see right away that their business was slowing down. My own sales weren't coming in as fast as I wanted, nor were they at a volume that would sustain their downturn. I was unhappy that even though I was out in the field selling, it still wasn't the type of sales position I really wanted; it was merely a beginning.

I began yet another search and interviewed with many different companies. One sales office in downtown Chicago used a headhunter to get a handle on candidates' abilities and personalities. I remember this fellow calling to tell me that I was a finalist for a certain position at a large company, and to meet him at his office. As we traveled together by cab to the company's sales office, he finally revealed what had, until then, been meant to be a secret: I was up for a position at H.S. Crocker. At the Crocker sales office, I spent an hour talking with the manager, Albert Trice, and then I was told that I would be notified of Trice's decision later in the week. Since I was still employed by the direct mail printing company, I was not overly concerned about whether or not I would receive a job offer. I still had plans to interview with other companies.

It wasn't long, though, before I received a call offering me the job. The main stumbling block was that the job entailed frequent travel to Wisconsin, as well as covering all of Chicago and its surrounding areas. I turned the job down, telling Mr. Trice that I just couldn't leave my wife alone for long periods. About a week later, he called again and offered to make some compromises regarding the travel schedule—I would only be gone a few days a month. This time, I said I would think about it.

Because God works in mysterious ways, in the latter half of the two-year period I worked for the direct mail company, they lost a large account that forced both plant, production, and sales layoffs. Being the low man on the totem pole, I was out of a job first. By that time, Darla and I were married and in the process of adopting our first child. Now it became extremely important that I make every possible effort to ensure a good life with every opportunity for our new baby. Later, with the addition of our adopted daughter, the stakes would go up even higher. Darla was doing her part at home, I was doing mine, and we both devoted all we had to success as a family.

Now I didn't have time to leisurely scout out a new position; I needed a job in a hurry. My decision was easy. I immediately returned Trice's call and told him I would gladly take the job. Thank goodness the timing was perfect; he still hadn't filled the position. I chalk this one up to serendipity and the cosmos, once again, working in my favor. Within one week I was working again, only this time it was for H.S.Crocker, Co.—a place where I could finally see the road ahead.

To this day, Al Trice is an extraordinary friend and colleague, and serves on my own board of directors.

Of the many characteristics that make Ron Giordano successful, his tremendous intensity, planning ability, persistence, and creativity are outstanding. Every day Ron has a row of file cards on his desk, shingled in order of the phone calls he will make that day: calls to new and old customers, follow-ups to prospects, and who knows what else; but he will make all those calls. That's called planning!

Persistence: Ron came into my office one day, and smelled like rotten cheese. When I asked him about the odor, he acknowledged that he had been in a cheese prospect's basement where all of the aging cheese loaves hung from the ceiling and dripped all over the floor. After months of unsuccessfully trying to see the owner, Ron grabbed the only time he could with the prospect to talk about his label requirements. He got the order, smelly shoes and all!

Ron's creativity and innovative nature came to the fore when trying to open the account of a large pharmaceutical company. He was immediately faced with a great number of obstacles to satisfying their qualifying requirements for suppliers. Not to be discouraged, Ron befriended the Director of Quality Control, who spent months educating Ron on the procedures needed. He used the Director as a consultant on the necessary changes our plant had to make to comply with their specifications, and then Ron became their consultant with regard to how the company could improve its packaging, lower costs, and improve deliveries.

Ron has always invested his time and energies for the benefit of our customers; in turn, they have invested their full confidence that Ron will remove all risks in having our company as their supplier. It doesn't get any better than that!!!

Al Trice, employer, teacher, supervisor, and admiring friend of Ron Giordano.

As soon as I arrived at H.S. Crocker, I knew I'd hit the big leagues.

I had plenty to keep me busy. I had many products to sell, and had a universe of opportunities to take advantage of. Crocker was unique as compared with our competitors because not only did we operate five plants across the country, we also had a very long history in California, going back to 1856. Our corporate office was located in San Bruno, near San Francisco, where we produced food labels, folding cartons, travel brochures, postcards, and pharmaceutical labels. The other four plants produced similar products with the exception of the Chicago plant, which produced foil lidding for yogurt containers.

I realized just how vital this multi-product line was (and still is) to the company's success. I must have looked liked a toddler at Disneyland the first time I took the tour. With each direction I looked, I saw something new and exciting (even magical!) for a born salesman like myself. No fooling: I had a tingle running up and down my spine and butterflies in my stomach. Chatting with Darla one night around the time I began at Crocker, I realized that those are necessary emotions if you really want to make it in sales, or any other field, for that matter. The truth is, you must be so pumped up and believe so strongly in what you are selling, that it will inspire your clients to purchase whatever you may suggest to them. That was a very important tool for me to pick up.

At H.S. Crocker, I found my niche, along with an opportunity to grow. I wasn't concerned about promotions because I knew then what I know now: a good salesperson is worth his weight in gold to an employer. Eventually, I became known at the company as the "entrepreneur," the guy who would push the creative envelope and challenge the plants to do better. My focus was on bringing in new business. In some cases, that meant pushing the plants to learn how to produce a label even if it had never been produced that way before. I was creating a competitive position, after all. Each of the five plants were producing orders for me as I sold the entire H.S. Crocker product line. This gave me credibility and it also gave me something even more important at the time: I gained the attention of each and every plant manager and production manager. It wasn't too long before they were eager to talk to me, and eventually, they were as enthusiastic as I was about my new ideas and producing them, as it meant more volume for their plants as well. If I could be aggressive in offering new ideas and new concepts with plants eager to produce, I could keep the competition off guard. By being creative and pushing the envelope, the plants began to follow suit, testing their skills and enjoying the ability to go where no one else had gone before. In fact, before long, we were all embracing the concept of "pushing the envelope."

My first assignments were very tough. I was given a territory and four existing accounts with a base volume of $100,000 ($25,000 for each account). When I went to see the first customer, he informed me that he had just filed bankruptcy, but I didn't let it get me down. The second customer told me that all purchasing was being moved to the East Coast, and that their local facility would now only be used for manufacturing. "Okay," I said to myself, "keep pushing!" The third client reported that he was closing down operations and pulling out of the business. Then, to top it off, the fourth client told me his volume was lower than it had been in years. Of these first four clients, I saw my base sales and potential for growth in these accounts evaporate before my eyes. It was not an auspicious start, but as usual, I wasn't going to give up that easily. I knew that right out of the gate, I had to make it happen, some way, somehow.

I guess I did manage to convince myself, because during my first year, I achieved a total of $350,000 in sales coming from all four of our plants, mostly with new businesses. The second year I jumped to $750,000, and the third year I set a record with H. S. Crocker and sold $1MM in sales—the first H.S. Crocker sales rep to accomplish this goal. By my fourth year, I was honored to receive a Sales and Marketing Executives Oscar Award, which does, by the way, look like an Oscar. From that point on, I continued to move up the sales ladder, winning contests and trips, and making Darla very proud.

Al Trice was one of those who referred to me as the "entrepreneur" because I was so bullheaded about finding solutions to problems (large and small), coming up with new concepts, convincing both clients and manufacturers to think big and think smart. I simply never gave up, no matter what. I always looked for (and almost always found) another way to make something happen, even when everyone else was scratching their collective heads. I spent hours searching for leads in trade magazines, contacting machinery manufacturers, and reaching out to any source I could find among packaging engineers. I also wanted my customers to remember me—I wanted to stand out. Using my graphic art and design background to come up with creative ideas, I infused products with life so that the customer or prospect felt we were really doing something unique and special—something just for them.

It occurred to me over and over again that building a successful life and career was all in the details, the seemingly little things. During those years, I created a system I've kept in place ever since. It sounds simple enough, but results don't always come from arduous work— sometimes it's a matter of research, organization, follow-through or a simple brainstorming session—an idea that hits you—bang!—while brushing your teeth or mowing the lawn. Whenever I came across a prospective client, customer, or job lead, I'd write all pertinent information down on a 3" x 5" index card so that when I made a follow-up call, I had all the information I needed right in front of me. This simple system of index cards let a prospect or client know that I actually cared about the details. My aim was to be as persistent as possible (without ever being rude or impolite), and never, ever allowing myself to "let one go." Naturally, there were times when I thought I was just spinning my wheels, but I told myself over and again, "Don't let go, keep pushing, you can do it!" Amazingly enough, those index cards probably helped me make more sales than any other single thing, and they continue to do so.

I also always try to meet with someone face to face rather than by telephone or e-mail. More than once, in the dead of a Midwest winter, preparing to drive one hundred miles or longer, I would think, "Maybe I should just make some phone calls from the office." Instead, I'd persevere because I knew it was almost always worth the trip. And it taught me something very important: just when you think you're out of gas, you'll miraculously find a source to refuel. I worked extremely hard to keep myself motivated. After awhile, I found it became automatic. Even more remarkable, I found the feeling was returned in kind. I enjoy my clients very much because it seems that for every random act of kindness or effort on my part, they are just as happy to return the favor.

With every week, month, and year that passed, I saw my work pay off with the greatest return possible, not only in my business life, but in my personal life as well. It was clear to me by the time I reached 30 that whatever I put into any situation was what I would take away. No matter how hard or time-consuming, my efforts would pay off and I would reap the benefits. Were my efforts always successful? Of course not. Nothing is guaranteed in this life, but I learned that I could make the wheel of fortune spin my way, as long as I didn't lose sight of my goals. I was able to move up at H S Crocker so quickly by setting goals and by meeting them.

My "toolbox of success" was almost complete (though it's never fully complete because there's never an end to learning). I had within me a gift that I wasn't using to its greatest potential, though. In 1985, on a whim, I decided to audition for a local radio station in downtown Chicago—The Chicagoland Radio Information Center. The non-profit station broadcast 365 days a year, around the clock, specifically for the visually-impaired and blind community. When I read the script aloud, they claimed to love my voice. I knew I had that rich basso profundo inside me, but I had begun to play it down. Mostly, it just elicited giggles from the family, who referred to me as "the Voice." I won the audition and began co-hosting a one-hour live show every Friday morning with a woman who was an author, reporting local news and current events. After a while, I suggested branching out and doing other types of informative programming—again, I was always moving, always thinking, always racing forward, except when enjoying my evening glass of wine.

I had an acquaintance—a buyer for a pharmaceutical company—who loved to cook and her food was fantastic. Enthusiastic about helping the blind learn to cook, she agreed to do a recorded show on Saturdays. Another frequent guest, Dr. Camille, was also a huge success amongst our listeners. As a psychic reader with clients all over the world, she continues to amaze, both in her accuracy and her generosity. Our live call-in shows drew many, many listeners.

Someone once accused me (probably rightfully so) of being a Romanticist as I always ended my programs with a poem, sometimes by my own pen. That's when the "Voice" began to manifest itself. Lost in the poetry, my mind caught up in the words and ideas, my voice deepened and became richer. I didn't know it then, but as the months and years went by, I would learn to count on my "broadcast voice" for a little extra drama, and as a method of commanding my listeners' attention. My family teased me about it, but I knew the truth—it actually showed up in the monthly sales statements—I was outselling myself with this new persona! I soon came to rely on my oratorical skills as a crucial part of my sales presentation.

It had taken me a relatively short period of time to contact and recruit my radio guests, and very little effort, but according to the calls and letters we received daily, my actions had brought so much to so many. It is a feeling that is hard to describe. It's not that I felt superior—God forbid—it's that I felt deeply satisfied. It made no difference if a person was sighted or not, it didn't matter in the least if my listeners couldn't see. What really mattered was how we all felt. It was about a random act of kindness for an often overlooked community of people.

Obviously, we conduct business in a business-like fashion, but there is always room for compassion and sensitivity, regardless of the forum. The happiness I experienced by delivering happiness to others translated into my sales career perfectly—I knew that if I could help a listener feel good about themselves, I could help a client feel good about themselves, too. Happiness breeds success and I was lucky enough to recognize that early on.

I had started at H.S. Crocker in July 1970, and within a couple of years, my sales grew from $3MM to $4MM annually—I had two customer service representatives working on my orders alone. Soon after, the Chairman of the Board took me to lunch and asked me to take over one of the company's plants that was hemorrhaging money. He asked what my plan might be for turning things around. I advised that in order to really straighten the mess out, we'd have to sacrifice $500,000 the first year, we'd break even in the second year, and we'd be back in the black by year three. He thought it to be a sound plan, but he told me later he thought I'd beat my own prediction. He knew I was always pushing the envelope, always challenging the plants to do more and to offer new products. I was able to get away with my renegade tactics because I had the sales, profit, and track records to prove my case.

After revamping the plant, we broke even the first year and then continued to make money every year afterward. I advanced from salesperson to General Manager, then to V.P. General Manager, on to Executive V.P. before being named President, and then to Chairman of the Board and President/CEO—all the while burying my nose in index cards and pushing my plants for more and better, because my clients trusted me and I wasn't going to let them down.

Just recently, I was very proud to receive the Chicagoland Entrepreneurial Award, which I shared with my own family and the families of my co-workers. Awards are wonderful things to receive, but the most wonderful thing of all is enjoying the results of your personal success and how they have not only added to your life, but to the lives of others. You may have a plaque to hang on your wall, but if you really believe in yourself and what you do for your customers, you already know what success is. You don't really need that award for all to see, but it sure feels good when you are already aware of your God-given gifts.

Yes, there are days for all of us when we'd rather crawl under the desk and hide from the never-ending stresses of work. Problems at home or with the children can turn your life upside down. We all know that adversity, whether minor or devastating, will rear its ugly head from time. Adversity will affect all of us differently and it will always leave a scar, albeit perhaps a small one; it will also affect how we behave. When he was just nine years old, my son was involved in a terrible accident when he was hit by a car outside our home returning from the karate lessons he loved. Thankfully, he recovered, though those days and nights were amongst the most difficult of our lives. Our daughter had her share of scares and tears, too. It's almost impossible not to let some adversity cross over into your work. Most importantly, though, we dealt with everything as a family. My wife and I had to maintain our composure; she had to keep the home and care for the kids, and I had to work, usually 60-70 hour weeks at the time. It was hectic, frightening, and frustrating, but the bad times always passed. In fact, it has occurred to me as I've gotten older that God, or the Powers That Be if you will, test us with adversity to help us become wiser, stronger, and more flexible.

Sometimes we lose our greatest assets—our employees and colleagues. I lost some terrific managers and salespeople myself along the way, but I learned that with each obstacle and feeling of despair, I had to look ahead and say to myself, "Self, everything happens for a reason." I could never replace the business relationships and friendships I had with these marvelous people, but I could never lose the lessons I'd learned by example from them. I like to think that we simply took different courses in life because that was our destiny, and these good folks had followed their instincts just as I had. If there's one great lesson I've learned about adversity, it's the ability to become adaptable under any and every situation. Whether the problem is a shortage of material for customers to power shortages to working with new employees, we all continue on because no one and nothing is perfect. We have no choice but to accept the ground rules and play the game. That means putting in honest effort every day, along with a determination to be great no matter what it is you do—to be proud of your accomplishments because no one can ever take them away from you.

PART TWO

The Basics

CHAPTER THREE

· · · · · · · · · · · · · · · · · · ·

Are You Really Right for Sales?

So, what do you want to be when you grow up? Really…if you could work at anything you'd like, what would it be? It used to be that men would find a trade of some kind, or if the family had money, they'd go to University. Sadly, many men and women had few to no options and took whatever job would pay them a minimal wage. Up until the last century, a man might follow his father into business and then pass it on to his own son, usually whether he liked it or not. A poor man working for someone outside the family had little chance of ever being promoted and retired, or he was fired when he was deemed too old or feeble to keep up with difficult, physical work.

Thank goodness things have evolved and we have many, many more options open to all segments of the population. Most occupations don't require great physical skills now. Most parents prefer to see their children make their own life choices. Now, if you find yourself unhappy with a job, you can simply look for another. In fact, even a spontaneous change in career can help you find your correct path. Be forewarned, though: changing jobs on a whim is not the way to go. My incentive to change jobs until I was hired by H.S. Crocker was motivated by my entrepreneurial yearnings, but when my responsibilities grew with a wife and children, I was very appreciative of steady, stable work. My father had set a fine example for me, but he'd also encouraged me to find my own way.

I've heard sales referred to as a "stop-gap" gig, something to do when you don't know how to do anything else, or when you're between jobs. I say that's a bunch of nonsense. In some circles, salespeople are amongst the best paid and most essential people in an organization, especially if it means a nice commission on a big-ticket item. Salespeople must have a very well-honed set of talents, regardless of what anyone has told you. As in any career, though, you must usually pay your dues before you start climbing the ladder.

You may not need a degree to go into sales, but you'd better be sharp or you'll fail.

Clearly, you've picked this book up because you want to learn how to be successful. But what is success? What is this nebulous thing we chase so wildly over the course of most of our lives? We take risks and we make mistakes; sometimes we leap before looking, and sometimes we make detailed plans. I suppose there are people who don't care about being successful, or perhaps they define the word in an alternative way. My definition of success is: focusing on what you have set for a goal and giving everything you can to fulfill that goal. Setting a goal isn't easy because it demands determination on your part, as well as understanding what good and bad choices are. It also requires cooperation and understanding from the people around you. You need support in order to thrive, so be sure to include—or even recruit—as many sources of support as you can amongst your friends, family, and colleagues, then keep the lines of communication open. Let your support system know that when you enjoy success, they will share in the benefits.

In many cases, including my own, you may have set a goal without even knowing it. Maybe you've been dreaming of a certain path in life since you were in kindergarten. Perhaps your family has influenced some of your life choices, perhaps certain opportunities simply fall into your lap, and sometimes you need to do some deep soul searching. My goal reared its head over and over in my childhood and young adult years, making itself impossible to ignore. I'd go so far as to say that my goal made itself known with my rigged-up hot dog stand before I was ten years old.

Regardless of how your goal emerges, the most important thing is to stay the course and keep your vision set precisely on what you want to achieve. In sales, that means making contact, getting the order, and knowing that you've satisfied a client to the best of your ability. Achieving success means both remembering and combining the things you've learned along the way—and you never stop learning. In the end, it's the combination of your intimate knowledge of the product (or whatever it is you are selling), along with the discipline it takes to do things and meet people you'd sometimes rather not. Those qualities will help you to stand apart from the others time after time.

A top-notch, stunningly successful businessperson may have an MBA from one of the finest learning institutions in the country, or he or she may have no formal education whatsoever. What really matters is that regardless of your background, you attain success through drive and determination. Getting there isn't easy, but then again, nobody said it would be. A degree hanging on your wall doesn't earn you the right to be successful; that right is earned by gaining respect from your clients and by always employing up-front, honest business ethics. That's what will help make you stand out in the crowd as well. Sometimes, simply offering a client or prospect a great deal will set you apart from the others—that's one trick. But a good buyer will also respect an honest approach above all else.

To all of you out there who didn't have the means to procure a business degree, this book is meant to give you confidence and to demonstrate that we, too, have an equal chance of success as our more educated colleagues. A degree won't inspire trust in your clients—you must earn that trust, and most of all, you must cultivate the ability to communicate with your customers, your prospects, and everyone else who crosses your path along the way. Remember: if you have the right tools and the proper outlook, you have the ability to do anything you want. You can find the tools right here; the outcome is up to you.

Maybe you've thought about attending one of the special classes or mail order sales programs that are advertised in the back pages of your local newspaper to learn the basics of good salesmanship. Perhaps like I was, you are simply drawn to sales, whether you mean for it to be a life-long pursuit or not. There are countless reasons to explore sales as a long, prosperous, and satisfying career, as long as you are willing to learn all you can and to really appreciate the fact that you have that knowledge. Think of the power of knowledge. The more you learn—the more familiar you become with every aspect of your line of products, your company, and yourself—the more power you'll enjoy. Your knowledge of every detail—from your competitor's prices to the way the product is manufactured, from your prospect's favorite kind of sandwich to your client's wife's birthday—results in a profound relationship with whatever it is you are selling! It helps you to develop such confidence in the product's performance that your enthusiasm then becomes contagious.

This is where success is bred, but it's up to you to find out which keys open your doors to success. Mine are my enthusiasm, my determination, my voice, my ability to communicate, my respect for all parties involved, and my excitement about thinking outside the box. Yours may be the same, some may be different and more suited to your field, and some will be uniquely yours. But you'll never find out if you don't experiment a bit.

Personally, I never took any classes, nor did I buy any books that professed to tell me exactly how to find success. Instead, through sheer determination, I did what I thought needed to be done. Don't get me wrong; books and education are wonderful resources. It's just that not everyone has access to the right ones. Some folks have priorities that outweigh the desire to obtain a degree. Fortunately, though, the sales field is not an elitist one. You do not have to be from the higher echelons of society to be great in sales. To be successful in sales you need perseverance, determination, and faith in yourself. Though the emphasis is on success in sales, the real message in this book supersedes and complements advice for would-be salespeople. If you do not have faith in yourself, you will simply spend your days driving from prospect to prospect, and leaving without a sale.

There is an adage that applies to just about everything: "You've gotta have the right tools." What are the tools that can take you to a higher level of success? I wrote this book to answer that very question—to help you understand what you need in order to succeed and to help you find the right tools to do so. It's up to you to create your own style to complement the tools you put to use. The qualities you need cannot be bartered or traded; you can't just go out and purchase them. Truth, knowledge, understanding, dedication, desire, and determination are innate qualities that you already possess; you just need to learn how best to use them.

I will never suggest that formal business training is unnecessary. Like everything else in life, formal training works well for some and not so well for others. If business training feels like a good fit for you, go for it, but then do something with it. If you prefer on-the-job training, there are opportunities for you as well. There are many successful people in the world who have made their way from nothing to something; they may not have had formal training, but they had common sense, worked their way up the ladder, and put in the effort to learn. If this is your way, then roll up your sleeves and put in the time. That doesn't mean working for eight hours, and then forgetting everything until you walk into the office the next morning with a hangover. The theory behind physical exercise is "no pain, no gain." In sales, pain today could mean joy tomorrow. Don't get hung up on not having a formal education; not everybody is so fortunate. Use what you have to work with: your natural enthusiasm, positive attitude, and belief in yourself, and build a foundation upon these qualities and what you have already accomplished.

If you have been fortunate enough to receive a formal business education, make that education work for you. Don't sit back and think that just because you have a piece of paper hanging on the wall you need not put forth any effort; often you must put forth even more effort because you do have that piece of paper. The other elements necessary for your success require you to develop and enhance your personal qualities, and without that effort, your degree will simply be a decoration on your office wall.

In sales particularly, it makes no difference whether you are formally trained or not. If you are successful and a proven producer, you will be looked upon and sought after as a valuable addition to any company.

When you make your first sale, or if you have a great sales call, you will know it was worth all the hard work you put into it. Your adrenaline will flow and you'll walk away feeling like you've just won the lottery. Don't dwell on past failures and opportunities missed. Just as in golf, after 17 bad holes, one perfect shot on the 18th makes the game a success. Enjoy your successful sales moments and then move on to the next goal, always remembering that you did it once and you can do it again.

Living in the Real World

There are many things to contemplate in choosing a career. First, you need to honestly explore your personality. If you are shy or timid, a person who is loathe to send their steak back because it's underdone, sales may be wrong for you. If starting up a conversation with a stranger makes you shiver with fear, sales may not be the wisest career choice. For me, there isn't a day that goes by that I don't go in search of at least 20 or 30 conversations, the more the merrier, be they with strangers or not. We all have "personality types" and while most of us can conquer our little fears, for others that fear is just too daunting to overcome. You must make a very honest assessment of your personality type before jumping into the field. If you don't take criticism well, you may want to look elsewhere. If you are your worst critic, that's a definite deal-breaker.

If you secretly believe that the product you are being asked to sell is ridiculous or useless, follow your instinct and run! You won't do right by yourself or by the company if you cannot find something beautiful, useful, or innovative in your product. If you really desperately want to be in sales, then be sure you believe in the product and company you are working for—I'm afraid you're pretty much doomed if you don't. It's just too hard to fake and a prospect will pick up on that immediately.

To be successful in sales, you must have a love for challenges. You might have a great day, and then the next day you might feel like you died and went to hell. This is not uncommon; we all suffer life's curveballs. The trick is to look for what the next day will bring with optimism. Leave the prior day behind you. Don't bring excess baggage along; it will only pull you down. Move, and by doing so, you will be gaining both experience and poise, both of which will make you a better salesperson. Instead of dreading them, look to challenges with excitement and your fear will disappear. We all face challenges every day—it's how we handle them that makes the difference. Imagine a golfer. He plays a great hole—either par or a birdie—and he's fired up for the next round. On the next hole, he double bogies and kicks himself for the mistake. Unless he's a terribly bad sport, he won't throw his clubs down and quit; instead, he goes on to the next hole with the anticipation (and expectation) that he'll do better. Your challenge is much the same.

Sales is no different than any other profession: you need to love what you do. You have to allow yourself to feel the energy flowing through your body when good outcomes result. To this day, I still feel the rush when I'm working on a project and it turns out to be a winner. I have never lost that love over the past 35 years. In fact, the more I do, the more I want to do. I can't wait for the next challenge, even if it doesn't go my way. In other words, you must be a person who isn't afraid of risk, who sees obstacles as challenges, and who can let your enthusiasm shine and be shared.

Presence and Communication

Let's make this very clear: mumblers need not apply. As an actor practices enunciation and voice projection, it wouldn't hurt any salesperson to do the same. If you're on a cold call, it's very unlikely that the receptionist will even let you through the door if you're whispering into your collar. Communication doesn't mean yelling at someone; it means speaking slowly and clearly and naturally—and with a smile. As I mentioned earlier in Chapter One, when I discovered my "Voice," I was amazed by the results. People treated me differently— with more respect. Even more importantly, they listened. Whether you are a brand-new salesperson or a weathered veteran, there always ought to be a spark in your voice and manner that makes you seem so confident, your client is moved to buy. Sometimes you need to feed that spark to get the fire going, and sometimes the fire burns brightly but needs direction. You learn how to direct your voice, your smile, and your mannerisms with time and practice, just like anything else.

To really enjoy your career as a salesperson, you must be willing to explore your presence, your character, how you come across on a first impression and onward. You need to shine when you present yourself to a client or prospect and you ought to be eager to learn how to constantly improve yourself, even if it means hours in front of the mirror. If you want to stand out, your charisma is your most important asset.

Your ability to communicate cannot be overstated. I would not have made it to the top if I was still pronouncing T's like D's. There's a lot more to it, though. You'll be communicating all sorts of detailed information to a wide variety of people, and naturally you'll want everything to go as you wish. You also need to learn to listen. We'll go into more detail in the next chapters.

The Family

It's not easy to build an account base and still have time for your family. Especially as the kids get older, there's baseball, football, soccer, cheerleading, drama productions and dozens of after school activities your kids sure would like for you to attend. Sometimes, to the delight or frustration of your children or your boss, you've got to make compromises with your time. You need teamwork at home; your significant other and you will have to make efforts to communicate and understand each other's needs. Sales can be more flexible than some other careers, but remember your priorities: if you are consistently canceling meetings to attend every game your kids play, you are taking advantage of your flexible hours and you are missing opportunities. The best act is a juggling act; it just takes a little patience and understanding. During the week, I work long hours at the office and in meetings with customers and prospects, but I made every effort to be home for dinner, just like my dad did. On the weekends, bring your cell phone so that you can make some quick calls during your son's karate class or your daughter's baseball games. Just like juggling, this takes practice. In some cases, compromise may mean finding a career that is more suitable for your family needs.

Love It or Leave It

Sales is a very unique profession with its own set of challenges and rewards. If you decide to become a salesperson, you must ask yourself if this is really what you desire. Sales involves a great deal of hard work; it's not just an exciting adventure full of travel, expense reimbursement, perks, commissions, and lunches with prospects. Can you handle the stress, tension, long hours, and eating alone on the road? Some days, you will find yourself waiting and restless, trying to find something to do to occupy your time. Sooner or later, though, you'll be so busy you'll need to remind yourself to breathe. You will enjoy some great experiences in sales, and I am not trying to discourage anyone from something they believe they can do well. My intention is simply to prepare you for all of the aspects of the job.

Over the years, you will develop your own collection of stories to tell. If you are the right person for the job, you will remember the situations that have made you what you are today. Like any other professional, salespeople always find a way to remember the good times. I truly hope that the tools I offer will help you find and maintain the good times, and that good fortune can pave its way through your life.

I went from salesman to CEO, rung by rung, fighting all the way. Bring on the obstacles, I say! How do I continue to feed that spark? With overwhelming enthusiasm and complete belief in myself. As noted earlier, enthusiasm is contagious and cannot help but light a spark in others. When your eyes light up, when your smile is authentic, and when you believe in what you sell, your energy excites others. Think about walking through a flea market. When you see something you really want, you begin the bargaining process. You want the best deal you can get, and your efforts are reinforced by the belief that you are capable of getting that deal. Is that belief any different than how you handle a sales transaction when calling a prospect? Not really!

So why not go into a prospect's office with that same confidence? You're not going to please every buyer, but you will never be ashamed of the effort you made. Have I liked or enjoyed working with every engineer, buyer, and director I've encountered? Hell, no! Sometimes I've wanted to stand in a guy's face and tell him to take a long walk off a short pier, or worse. Much better to maintain your composure, never allowing the other person to drag you down.

The sales field demands that you regiment your time and attention to detail. Make no assumptions and take nothing for granted. Can you get by without those efforts? Sure, but eventually you will be outsmarted by those who have employed a better business strategy. Don't fall into the trap of making six phone calls and then BSing with your pal on the seventh call. Believing in yourself means being persistent when calling customers or prospects from your office, making call after call after call and never stopping to check on the score of the game! It means being selfish with your time, but it also means you are guaranteed success.

Disappointment and Failure

I'll be very up-front: you need to prepare yourself, because the percentage of failure in sales is high. I have probably signed a mere one out of every twenty to thirty prospects. If you're the type to cry when people say "no," sales is not your forte. In my case, a simple "no" does not deter me at all. I have learned to work around rejection by continually adding to my list of potential opportunities. I never, ever stop seeking out opportunities—they are my lifeline. You cannot sit back and wait for things to come to you. You need to constantly be on the lookout for ways to slip in a pitch, to learn something new, to make a few phone calls, or brainstorm on improving a certain product. If you keep your eyes open, you'll find opportunities everywhere. A vendor may have a tip for you, or you might get a call from an engineer you asked to keep you in mind if something new were to arise. No matter what, keep on keeping on and don't give up the fight.

Regardless of the work you do in the world, you will always experience times of disappointment and failure. It's no different in sales. You may have put forth your very best efforts; you may have presented with energy and enthusiasm and had an absolute belief in your ability to sign a prospect, only to be met with disappointment. It's very important to maintain a healthy perspective on this; don't allow yourself to become discouraged easily. Never think of yourself as a failure; remember that each disappointment gives you a chance to reassess your approach, fine-tune your technique, and move on to the next challenge. Every day is a learning experience; learning from your failures will only make you more successful.

Your belief in yourself, coupled with enthusiasm and positive energy, will take you a long way in sales. Continually assess yourself to make sure you are projecting the confidence, energy, and enthusiasm you need to send the right message to clients and prospects, and you will find yourself rewarded with the success you desire. If after reading this chapter you have determined that you might not have the kind of personality best suited to sales, kudos to you for being honest with yourself. You're certainly not a failure as a person if sales isn't the right field for you. But be sure to pass this book along to anyone you know who might fit the bill!

CHAPTER FOUR

. . . .

Getting your Foot in the Door

Any mission you set out on—particularly when it's finding a great job—takes a lot of thought and planning beforehand, maybe more than you are aware. It's not easy these days (has it ever been?) to be noticed, to stand out in the crowd. Information bombards us from everywhere and once it's your turn in the spotlight, it's easy to come off as too arrogant or too timid. I say the best bet is to come armed with information. Competition is tough out there, regardless of the nation's economic status, and you need to learn the basics of an interview, but you also need to devise some method of ensuring that your interviewer remembers you above all the rest of the candidates he or she has seen in any given day. Bake a plate of brownies? Er…no. Advise in a confident tone of voice that you're the only candidate they should even consider? Not such a great idea. Remember, it is YOU you are selling and you can't count on anything but your skills, your knowledge, and your poise to make that lasting impression. On top of all that, you must make sure you are interviewing for a company you believe in—one whose products truly excite you, or could potentially light a fire in your gut.

Again, some things you can do to impress your interviewer are no-brainers: make sure your shoes match, no stains on your tie, maintain a pleasant attitude throughout your interview. Other things lie in the smallest detail, though they may make the greatest impression. In this chapter we'll discuss getting your foot in the door, making the very best first impression you can, and landing the job (if it feels right to you, too.) We'll touch on ideas for finding jobs in an economy that may be depressed, the realities of salary versus commission, and even some fashion tips as well, because nothing ought to be overlooked when you're looking for the ideal job for you.

There are a myriad of ways in which to find companies that are looking for salespeople. The Internet can provide a cornucopia of information, and the newspaper always has dozens of listings in the Help Wanted section. Relatives, friends, acquaintances, former colleagues, and neighbors should be enlisted—anyone could surprise you if you just think to ask. There's never any shame in trying to better your life, and asking folks you know to keep an eye out for you should cause you no embarrassment. Word of mouth carries a lot of weight these days, especially when employers are looking for people with built-in recommendations from someone familiar to the company. More than anything else, though, it's time to think "outside the box" and consider some of the suggestions below.

If you're in a jam and need to find work quickly, you're likely to accept the first offer that comes your way. The only danger there is that you'll fall into a rut and discontinue the search for your dream job. There's no rule anywhere that prevents you from trying to better your life whilst under someone else's employ. In fact, you may have an advantage as you'll have plenty of time to thoroughly explore your options. Ideally, if you do your homework, you can locate and land any job that inspires, excites, and motivates you even while you're working full-time elsewhere. Just like upgrading to a new house or car, you can certainly spend some time each week researching new prospects with the comfort of knowing you aren't in panic mode.

People go to great lengths to research schools for their children, they visit a number of gyms before joining, and they may spend a year or more searching for the perfect home. Why don't people research the job market they're interested in more carefully? I wonder if you took a survey of your friends and family whether anyone would answer, "Of course! It's just as important that I'm happy at my workplace as it is that they're happy with me." Very few job seekers take the time to pick and choose whom they will take an interview with. Instead, they simply jump at the first positive response. You may have already decided that you'd like to sell cars, or food, or home décor; perhaps you're open to a number of products. As I'll repeat many times throughout this book, your enthusiasm for what you're selling is absolutely key to your long-term success.

Before you schedule any interviews, make a list of "must haves" (flexible hours, limited travel), a list of "I'd like to have's" (close to home, good support staff), and a list of "must not's" (too big a bureaucracy, frequent travel, too low a salary). This will help to narrow your search and will ensure that no one experiences any unpleasant surprises in the future. Next, go to the library and look through trade and business magazines. Find companies you think you'd like to work for and research them carefully. There is a huge amount of public information available to anyone interested in taking the time to find it. Visit different company Web sites and familiarize yourself with the contents provided. Most companies post press releases and general news, along with full descriptions of the product lines they offer. Also, you can try doing a search for the company name to find any news articles published about them. Take notes so that during the interview you can demonstrate your knowledge about the company, including VIP names, product lines offered, and differences between that company and their competitors. Know your market! Any interviewer will take notice of the time and effort you've put in. Don't waste your time, or the time of a prospective employer, if you have doubts about the company or position you are interviewing for unless you simply like to practice interviewing!

Remember that many companies avoid advertising job openings in the newspaper. Instead, they rely upon word-of-mouth referrals, they promote from the inside, they use the Internet, or they employ "headhunters." If you have some solid experience, you may find that a headhunter is your best bet; just be ready to wait by the phone, maybe for a good long time, kind of like an actor waiting for her agent to call with that "big movie deal." A headhunter will meet with you, assess your skills (both personal and professional), and try to match you to a company who needs what you can offer. In most cases, headhunters are compensated by the company employing their services, so all you'll need to invest is some legwork. It should be noted, though, that headhunters normally work with jobseekers who have a fair amount of training and experience.

I heard a story about a fellow who, unable to get an interview with one of the large stock exchange companies in Seattle, worked out quite a creative and successful strategy for getting his foot in the door.

Knowing that most executives lunched in the lobby level restaurants, he used his last dollars to purchase a decent-looking suit and then he simply wandered the courtyard during the lunch hour, looking for the chance to strike up a conversation with the right person. Within two weeks, he had landed a mid-level position at Smith Solomon Barney. The point is, when you think you've tapped out your job market, think again. Most employers appreciate creative thinkers, anyway.

Your Relationship with the Product

We've talked a bit about enthusiasm and how a salesperson should always be pumped up, with a strong belief in their product. Ideally, a salesperson should absolutely love selling whatever it is they sell. If the product is in the stores and on the shelves, take a look at it. How does it compare to the competition? How will your individual personality help you sell this product to other people? Would you buy it? When you look at the product, does it make sense to you? Does it excite you, or are you just considering the big bucks you might make? Remember, the money will come, but you must believe in the product first. Some poking and probing will help arm you with the necessary information you'll need to stand out—to show that you care enough to do homework before presenting yourself to ask for a job.

Personally, during this preparatory process, I usually ask myself questions and think about all of the possible answers from a bird's eye view. If I look at a product, get excited, and feel like I can't wait to sell it, that tells me something important. That excitement is an inexplicable and magical aspect of the product. If you feel that exhilaration the moment you look at such a product, whether it be roofing materials, cosmetics, or medical supplies, nothing else will make a difference; once you believe in the product, your frame of mind and your body language will communicate to any customer that you believe in what you are selling, you believe in what it can do, and you're excited about the benefits that your customer will enjoy with the product. If the product is unfamiliar to you, your research will have to wait until you have an opportunity (most likely during the interview) to ask questions and form the best opinion you can with the information available. If that "spark" never reveals itself, don't force the impossible. If you can't

stand behind the product you're selling, you'd best know right now that, ultimately, you will fail or worse, you'll eventually be fired for lack of sales.

Before the Interview

Once you've landed an interview for what seems to be the perfect job and product for you, you'll need to prepare a few important items if you haven't already. You'll need:

- A business card
- A newly updated résumé with referrals
- Any letters of recommendation

You ought to carry these items in a nice folder, hopefully inside a smart-looking briefcase. Even if this is your first time out, your business card ought to communicate consummate professionalism. Keep it simple with your name and contact information. Please leave your artsy side at rest: no smiley faces, flowers, fancy colors, or inspirational quotes. Some outfits will provide you with 100 or so free business cards, hoping you'll order more in the future. Unfortunately, these cards are almost always of a poor quality, with thin paper and superfluous information about the printing company on the back. In plain words, they look cheap and they detract from your professionalism. Your business cards represent you—make sure they are clean and elegant.

Résumés come in many different styles. I suggest picking up a book or searching the Internet for examples of appropriate résumés. It's a good idea to create several résumés to suit several types of businesses. For example, if you are interviewing for a job selling foodstuffs, you may want to change your résumé slightly from the one you'll use when you go to interview for the auto sales job. It doesn't take much time, especially now that we have the technology to create 100 résumés and store them on the computer. I guarantee that taking steps like these will boost your confidence because you'll know you've gone above and beyond what most job applicants will do.

One very important piece of advice? Please don't lie, or even exaggerate, on a résumé, even in the smallest of details. Men and women in the highest echelons of politics and business have been fired for such

transgressions. It's always better to be honest and win people over with your smile, enthusiasm, and knowledge of the product, even if you lack experience. Your résumé should include a list of entries that are germane to the job you seek. If you are interviewing at IBM, your stint as a master chef at Taco Bell is best left off. Instead, if you don't have much work experience, concentrate on anything in your past that relates to technology or computers, sales, or people skills. The same goes for referrals. Employers DO check, and if you're caught in any sort of shenanigans, like listing your mother as your last employer, your name will be mud, and mud creeps and slithers into every corner and crevice. Soon, you'll find yourself unable to get an interview anywhere.

Reassess Your Personal Appearance

Over the years, often while waiting in lobbies, I have seen salespeople who literally looked like something the cat dragged in. No one expects you to wear coattails to your interview—or eventually when calling on a prospect or customer—but it will make a difference if you are well groomed and dressed like you care about the impression you make. Not everyone can afford a closet full of Armani, but a clean and pressed shirt, slacks, and a sport coat can go a long way toward presenting yourself like a professional. Ladies have more options, but simple rules should include nothing overtly provocative, nothing worn or soiled, and nothing "over the top." When you feel good in a great outfit, you'll communicate self-esteem and attention to detail. Even if you know that the company you are interviewing for has a casual dress policy, make sure you look snappy during the initial interview—it shows you take your job seriously and that you respect your would-be employers. It's better to be clean and conservative than "hip," unless you are applying for a "hip" position. If you are interested in working for Banana Republic, you might consider wearing their fashions, for example. That's also where your research can come in handy. A good rule to follow is: good grooming + common sense + research = your best look for any given interview.

Commission vs. Salary

Loving your job is one thing; making a living is another. Before you interview, if possible, you might like to find out the means of payment the particular company employs. If not, be prepared to discuss the various options available. I have always been a believer in a base draw against a commission. The base pay is the amount you need to get by, so that you're not living in poverty. Of course, we're not talking about a brand-spanking new salesperson receiving a draw of 60M without a proven track record. But, if you feel you can do the job, the money will take care of itself.

A commission over and above the draw can be ideal, as it consistently gives salespeople a "sky's the limit" attitude; they can earn as much as they can sell. To me, a salary alone provides no incentive to earn more, to be more successful. I think that managers, too, should earn bonuses over and above their salaries so that they'll be sure to participate in the sales department's success. The best commission arrangement is earning a percentage of sales as well as a percentage of gross profit; the salesperson is rewarded for the sale, and the higher the gross profit, the higher the commission.

In a situation where there is a high-volume account with which gross profit is more difficult to attain, then I suggest a second program with a lower percentage for sales and gross profit. Both the salesperson and manager agree to acquire this piece of business, but the account is kept separately in the books so as not to destroy the earnings of all the other accounts with higher gross profits. You can identify these accounts as "contract" or "special accounts" on the accounting side.

Determining the method by which you will be paid is of tremendous significance as regards your actual income. The support of your manager becomes an important factor; it shows that your time and energy is not only important to the company and your earning, but also to the plant that is producing the order, for they also absorb some of the cost, along with the potential benefit you bring as a salesperson. Your manager should understand this complete scenario and should recognize your concerns. Be sure your immediate supervisor understands your potential, and how each payment option will affect you before any final decisions are made.

The Interview

You are, obviously, selling yourself during an interview. But that's not all—this is also your opportunity to learn more about the company and its products by asking questions. Preparing a list of questions may be useful, but conversation during an interview may take many twists and turns. You need to walk into that interview with as much knowledge about the product and the people you hope to be working with as possible. That way, you can ask direct, intelligent, and specific questions. For example, what type of training or assistance will you receive? Will the training continue as you begin to sell? What kind of support will you receive from your employer? Compile the answers to take home with you. If you're interested but need some time to think it over, ask the employer if the two of you can meet again after you have had a chance to digest all of the information.

Your interview is your chance to show yourself at your very best. Be sure to look at your interviewer directly. Shifty eyes convey a lack of confidence and honesty. Don't stare at your shoes, and for heaven's sake, smile! You need not change your personality—be yourself. If you try to be someone you're not, the results could be disastrous; like an actor who has forgotten his lines, you could easily end up stuttering and sputtering, red in the face and wishing to flee the premises immediately. People who interview job candidates understand that a job interview can be nerve-wracking, but especially in the sales field, you want to demonstrate confidence, enthusiasm, and good people skills. If you don't possess those qualities already, you may be on the wrong career path.

Reading your interviewer means staying very focused on the non-verbal messages he or she is sending you. If your interviewer is a burly man of over six feet, you can feel confident about giving a very hearty handshake; not so if your interviewer is a petite woman, in which case your handshake should be firm, but not overpowering. Once you master the art of reading someone, you will always work at an advantage. If your interviewer is the quiet type, don't feel pressed to fill silence with chit chat about sports or the weather. On the other hand, if he is ebullient, go ahead and speak up, being careful not to forget that this is a job interview. Use humor or a casual tone only if you feel sure it is absolutely appropriate. Speak in a polite tone, enunciating your words carefully.

I've found that most people who do hiring appreciate an interviewee who is upbeat, friendly, communicative, and most of all, keen to learn, so never be timid about asking questions. If you are the candidate who knows the most about the company and its products, and you are able to communicate that effectively, you are likely the candidate who will be chosen. Research never goes to waste. Even if you don't use what you've learned immediately, a time and place will no doubt present itself in the future. The very fact that you own knowledge (because no one can ever take it from you) will help you to stand out in the crowd of applicants. Be careful, though! Never correct your interviewer and take care not to appear to be a "know-it-all," but an "I'm willing to learn-it-all" type.

CHAPTER FIVE

∙ ∙ ∙ ∙ ∙ ∙ ∙ ∙ ∙ ∙ ∙ ∙ ∙ ∙ ∙ ∙ ∙ ∙ ∙

The ABC's (and Four D's) of Good Salesmanship

As in any profession, there are some basic elements in the sales field with which you must be familiar. Whether you are simply considering a career in sales, just starting out, or working as a seasoned veteran, understanding the basics will provide you with the necessary frame of reference for the work you'll be doing. As you become engaged in the more complex issues of sales work, understanding and incorporating these basic elements will provide the context you need to continue moving onward and upward.

Encouraging slogans like "do your best," "work hard," and "stay positive" have pretty much lost their value as they go into one ear and out the other, especially when they come from a parent, a teacher, or a boss. We understand exactly what they mean, but they've lost their punch over the years. There's a reason why certain adages are repeated over and over, though—it's because they really do work. If I may be indulged, I'd like to take a new look at some outdated notions. When you've successfully landed a job with a company you have faith in—because you did your research and wowed the powers that be— it's time to refocus and concentrate on how you can be the most successful salesperson you can be. The following are some notions that may have lost their bite over the last few decades, but reconsidered, they will absolutely make the difference between a mediocre job and a spectacular career. Even if you haven't gotten your foot in the door yet, these ideas are everlasting and never lose their value. Read them, understand them, live them, and you won't be disappointed.

Attitude: Energy and Enthusiasm

My most important tools, hands down, are positivity and enthusiasm. An upbeat, cheerful attitude can be the most contagious and advantageous quality you possess, too. The tone of your voice, your smile, and your own genuine excitement about the product you are selling will be seen by your boss as qualities you are likely to bring to your clients as well. Think positive, envision positivity, remain positive, and your presentation will surely be positively received. Always present yourself with energy to spare! Others can't help but sense the fire you carry, and by extension, you will carry that same fire to the company's clientele and prospects. Your attitude in general sends a signal louder than a freight train: you believe in the quality and the dependability of your product, as well as your company, and you will come through, come hell or high water! Your attitude about your product, your work, and yourself will always be evident to clients and prospects. The beauty of your attitude is that it belongs to you; it can always be developed, enhanced, and modified. You are responsible for cultivating the manner in which you appear to others. In sales, few things are more important.

The more positivity you can project, the better you convince a client or prospect that your product is of such high quality, they'd be crazy not to invest in it. As a salesperson, you absolutely must put forth the human effort needed to send this message. You may have a great Power Point presentation, impressive color brochures, or magnificent overheads, but do you possess the critical human element? The ability to talk to other people with radiant energy? You don't have to jump up and down and wave your arms about to get the message across, but you do need to demonstrate an absolute belief in the product and the services your company can provide.

It is all too obvious when someone is bored, lacks confidence, or doesn't care about their work; clients and prospects pick up on that immediately. Regardless of how your day is going, whether or not you feel discouraged, or would simply rather be somewhere else at that moment, you must push those feelings aside and adjust your attitude so that energy and enthusiasm shine through, every time you go on a sales call.

The Four D's (and an R)

The "Four D's," as I've come to think of them, are so important that regardless of whatever other qualities or skills you possess, you simply will not be able to move forward without them. Whether you're facing a challenge, dealing with potential disappointment, or realizing great success, the Four D's—Dependability, Dedication, Determination, and Desire—all shape your path as a salesperson.

Many of my friends are good card players and gamblers. I am not, but when it comes to the challenge of business, that's my game of chance. A salesman from one of my suppliers once said, "Ron's a tough negotiator, but he has to be. He's standing up for his employees and his company. Whatever he tells you is truthful, but he expects you to buckle down and work hard as a supplier, just as his customers expect him to buckle down for them."

Dependability

When you ask someone to put their faith in you, you must demonstrate that you are dependable, worthy of that faith, whether it's arriving on time for an appointment or remembering to carry the proper materials to a client meeting. That means doing your homework and being prepared for the next day before it begins. No matter whom you're meeting with—a business partner, a client, or a prospect—you will quickly lose face if you show you can't be counted on. You may think you can fool some of the people some of the time, but most people will pick up on a lack of dependability in the blink of an eye. If you did not learn this character trait at home or somewhere else along the way, it's time to evaluate yourself and think about making some changes. Change is never easy, but you must find a way to rise above the self-ishness of immediate gratification and learn to be the kind of business associate people know they can trust, any time or day of the week.

How do you demonstrate dependability? Stop for a moment and think about your daily life. How do you handle things like paying your bills or keeping promises? Can your neighbors depend on you to return a borrowed item, or do they warn the folks across the street not to lend you anything? We all backslide from time to time. It's easy to get into the habit of putting things off until tomorrow; unfortunately, tomorrow quickly becomes today, and you find yourself woefully unprepared. Here's the good news: you can take control of your life and make an honest effort to handle your responsibilities. This book can help, but ultimately, it's up to you to dig down deep and change some of the immature behaviors you haven't outgrown yet. We all have the ability to behave dependably on a consistent basis.

There are plenty of ways to learn to become dependable. Write notes to yourself to help you remember the things you need to do. Use whatever computer aids you have available to you; they don't have to be high-end tools—even the simplest computers or cell phones come equipped with day planners. You will see results if you force yourself to get organized. Plus, you'll find that when you become more accountable, your self-confidence will grow, and that will be obvious to everyone around you. Who do you want customers to see when they look at you: a person they can trust and depend on for help, or a person who clearly needs help himself? Let customers see the person you're striving to become—a dependable person worthy of anyone's business.

You need your customers to know that if they call you, you'll follow up and get back to them soon. An example of undependable behavior is to hide under the radar and avoid returning calls—you will lose the trust you've worked so hard to gain. Instead, take the bull by the horns, see to it that you take care of your customers, and always get back to them promptly. Don't pawn follow-up calls onto your customer service representative or anyone else; that's the easy way out and it will send the wrong message to your customers. Even if you don't have an answer for a particular client, your consistency in following up will pay off because you've shown you can be trusted simply by responding to them, even if it's to tell them you're still working on a solution.

Think about it this way: if you call a company to do some work around your home and they make a commitment to come at a certain time, you expect them to be there at the designated time. If they don't keep that commitment, you are left hanging. Particularly if you've left work early or made special arrangements to meet them, if they don't fulfill their promise, you're going to be steamed and you have every right to be. The problem with so many companies today is that everything is computerized; voice prompts take the place of a living, breathing human. As a consumer, does that leave you with the feeling that you are valued? When an establishment has a real person answering the phone, you may be directed to leave a message, but it's somehow more comforting than dealing with robots. Nor do I understand why the use of automated customer service is considered more efficient. In most cases, twenty pre-recorded voice prompts are required to find one simple answer. Especially in this day and age, when so few companies have real people answering and placing calls, it becomes all the more impressive when you are one of the live ones.

Why am I so hung up on dependability? Because so many companies and salespeople have lost the crucial quality of simply being human. Nothing created from a machine can ever replace a human telling you that he or she can be depended upon. In today's world, taking a personal interest already puts you ahead of so many others in the same field, just as it will in tomorrow's world. You can make all the difference simply by demonstrating dependability. The essence of dependability is to say what you honestly can do and then follow through with the same unwavering honesty.

Dedication

Not too many years ago, people were dedicated to the companies they worked for and stayed with them until retirement. Now, our world has changed and that doesn't happen much; yes, some people still approach their professions as lifelong careers, but certainly not to the same extent as in the past. If you want to be successful in your profession, you must be dedicated to it. You must love it, believe in it, and have the energy needed to accomplish all of the daily, seemingly mundane, tasks.

Being dedicated is about finding a path you love, and then taking all the time necessary to consistently improve your skills. I'm not talking about a nine-to-five job where you're simply putting in the hours until it comes time to collect your Social Security checks each month. I'm talking about really making a difference when you perform the duties assigned to you by your employer. No matter how menial the task may seem to you, you simply must do your very best because that task is important to someone. We all have different levels of performance, and it makes no difference if someone else is better than you at any given task. After all, there will also always be someone who is worse! What counts is your commitment and dedication to the duties at hand. No matter what task you've been asked to work on, believe in what you are doing and give one hundred percent of yourself towards accomplishing that goal, regardless of how much importance you assign that task. Dedication is as golden a character trait in the eyes of your clients as it is to your employer, and one day, perhaps when you are least expecting it, you'll be handsomely rewarded.

Determination

This is an area where many people fail because it is far easier to give up than to be persistent and determined. If you are a salesperson who lacks persistence, then sales is not the career path for you. In sales, you must find a balance between being determined and persistent without being obnoxious. After you have accepted an assignment from your boss or an order from a client, instead of groaning or pouting, you must resolve immediately that you have the confidence to do it and do it well, and then you must make it happen. It's by no means easy, and you cannot be a bully or a pain in the butt; instead, you must always strive to be professional and courteous no matter whom you are working with. Your follow-up, attention to detail, and ongoing attention to your customer or prospect will be rewarded when you demonstrate determination on a consistent basis.

Sometimes you'll have to wait for any pay-off or recognition. How long? You never really know; but persistent follow-up can go a long way as you'll soon learn. Check in with your customers from time to time to ask if there is anything you can do to help—and it's important to use those words verbatim—you don't want to make a pest of yourself, you'd just like to know if you can be helpful in any way. Customers need to know you are there for them, and sometimes they need to be reminded. The day will come when they call you, simply because you were always there for them, offering your help and services. Keep good notes, make a file for each customer (and each prospect, as well) and above all, be organized so that when you and your customer speak, you are always on the same page. When you begin your day, don't take the easy way out and leave something you'd rather put off for tomorrow—if it's on your calendar for today, do it today. There are no shortcuts if you intend to be a true success. Some people believe that they are determined; it's just that nothing is working. In my view, that means you're not determined enough. Customers and prospects can sense when you lack determination—they can smell it from a mile away. Buyers today are usually very sophisticated and can tell a swordfish from a minnow. Don't be a minnow! Present yourself as an intelligent, professional salesperson who believes in what you are selling. Be determined to demonstrate that your company can offer not only a better product, but a sales rep who can be relied upon no matter what.

Desire

We all have dreams and desires. When you were growing up, perhaps you wanted to be a pilot or work in a circus. Now you may have a desire to meet a life partner or travel to faraway places. It's very important that you live your life in the manner you have chosen. Desire takes us a long way in life; without desire, we would find no joy. What about you and your professional desires? You want a good job and you want to make a lot of money—we all do. If you apply that desire to your job, it can begin a domino effect: the more desire you have, the more goals you'll accomplish; the more goals you accomplish, the more money you'll make. Happiness isn't achieved with cash or material goods, but striving to quench a desire brings a sense of achievement that is highly satisfying.

Along the way, you must not lose sight of the customer's desires. Examples include a great product, a responsible and courteous sales rep, and the best possible prices. Couple your desires with those of your customers, and you'll do well. Even better, make this the hallmark of your presentation to prospects. When your client or prospect walks away with the feeling that they've "won," you've won, too.

From the time you were born, you've experienced desire: the desire to crawl, the desire to walk, the desire to be independent, and along the way, the desire to be successful. Life is basically one long list of desires and the methods we use to pursue our goals and dreams. I believe that the desire to succeed is the strongest desire most of us possess. Happily, it is one that can be fulfilled, but only if you're ready to work for it.

Responsibility

Although not one of the four D's, responsibility is also vital to your success. Being responsible is something we hear about every day. From the time we are young, we have certain obligations. If your mother asks you to feed the dog, it's your responsibility to do so. When you need something done well, you turn to the most responsible source you know. Just as you have responsibilities at home, on the job you are responsible to your clients and to the employer who is trusting you to fulfill the goals that have been set by all parties. In your professional career you have a responsibility to yourself, to your employer, to your clients, to all of the other people who are counting on you. Think about the people who work in every department of your company. Responsibility is a two-way street. The people who run the machines in your plant are responsible for producing a good product for both you and the customer. The customer is responsible for providing revenue. You are responsible for bringing in sales so that everyone can keep their jobs and support their families!

You are responsible for every action you take and every word you say in any interaction that takes place. It sounds a lot more daunting than it really is—you live your life this way already, whether you realize it or not. The important thing to remember is that people count on you—please don't let them down, for your sake, too. Being responsible means thinking about other people, having consideration for them, and being accountable for what you do and how you do it. In the end, being responsible will benefit you tenfold—not only in your job, but in how you conduct your everyday life.

There isn't one person—one employee—that doesn't deserve the best effort of the management team to work their hardest and to do their best to make a company successful. Everyone carries responsibility: the salespeople, the machine operators, the computer technicians, the receptionists, the janitors, etc. Ignoring any employee is the same as ignoring a puzzle piece—completion isn't possible. As you respect every individual around you, they will return the favor in kind. Keep focused and always be honest with the people who surround you. Above all, believe in what you do and believe in those who help you do it. That is your greatest responsibility.

Common Sense

Common sense plays a role in most aspects of our lives. It can play a role in honesty, appropriate etiquette, and remembering special information about your customers, for example. When all of these elements are part of your approach, pitching and closing the deal should come automatically.

Every salesperson really must use common sense in all arenas when working with customers and prospects. Simple honesty will go a long way toward convincing them that you can be trusted and relied upon. Basic appropriate etiquette is also part of the package. Remembering names is a common courtesy and thus is part of common sense. As we move further into the book, I'll expand on some great methods of putting common sense and common courtesy to use. Each element of common sense is important, but each alone is not enough. When they are combined into one package, backed up by the ideas brought forth in the Four D's, you will present yourself as a real person, not simply a salesperson. The customer will recognize you for who you are and will always feel comfortable working with you.

Under no circumstances will you be perfect. Fortunately, customers don't expect you to be perfect, but they do expect you to present well, have some business knowledge, and possess basic common sense. When you show yourself as that person, customers will feel comfortable working with you; they will understand that you are someone who will listen and act on their behalf. Especially when first starting out, you will not have the experience and prior knowledge to handle every situation. Even after over thirty years in the business, I come across new situations that I had not expected. This is when common sense is most important. No one knows all the answers, but if a customer knows that you can think on your feet and that you possess common sense, they will gain respect for you.

CHAPTER SIX

. . . .

Making Success Happen: It's Up to You

Taking the Time It Takes

We've covered some of the basic and general traits anyone, really, should incorporate into their professional (and personal) lives. Now let's move on to some of the things you can do to make sure your sales career grows and thrives. There are dozens of "tricks of the trade," and your attention and mastery of certain sales devices will make a significant difference, both in how you approach your job on a daily basis and, ultimately, how you achieve real success. I want to emphasize that many of these ideas are actions that every salesperson engages in—the difference is in the approach, in your level of enthusiasm, your belief in the product, and your willingness to commit yourself fully to your career.

Sales is very rarely a nine-to-five job. You're sure to be interrupted off-hours from time to time; you may have to excuse yourself from Sunday brunch once in a while to return a call; you may have to cancel going to the ballgame to take a meeting with a prospect; you may even have to postpone a vacation with the family. Is this unreasonable? Not if you want to be considered amongst the best in the business; not if you want to move up the ladder and keep your boss, your coworkers, and especially your clients and prospects happy because they know they're working with someone they can absolutely count on. Sales allows a lot of freedom—you aren't stuck in a cubicle day after day—but your clients may have operations that run every day, all day, and you should be prepared to be there if and when a client needs you. Show them your loyalty and availability and you'll eventually be rewarded with a referral, more orders, and an excellent reputation. The perks will come later if you're patient and very truly diligent in your work. Many of the perks are quite nice, too.

When I first started out in sales, a time which can be challenging and very frustrating, I made the decision to dedicate myself to a plan of persistent hard work, like my father before me and his father before him. By the time I was hired by H.S. Crocker, I kept myself busy digging up the names of potential clients, and I called and visited as many prospects as I could fit in a day. I didn't sleep much back then, but I was young and energetic with a growing family to feed. I operated on the premise that if I called on fifteen prospects, I would probably interest or sign just one of them. No matter the size of that one prospect, it was still a customer and that was golden. My eyes were peeled everywhere I went.

H.S. Crocker sold (and continues to sell) printed labels, foil lids, and booklet labels to the food and pharmaceutical industries. Walking down the aisles of the supermarket with my wife, I'd carry a pad of paper and a pen so I could take names off of containers, or addresses of different manufacturers—anything I could find that might turn into a lead. It drove poor Darla crazy, as a simple trip to the market became a grand treasure hunt for me. I could spend an entire day in the supermarket, something Darla prefers not to do. "Is this a ploy you've devised to avoid the honey-do chores?" she joked one day. Now, 35 years later, I leave her to do the shopping on her own time and this arrangement works out very well. In fact, today, Darla comes home and gives me names off containers to give to my sales personnel! She understands well now how important it is to keep looking for leads so that my salespeople can get their feet in the door.

During those early years in sales, I didn't limit my search to supermarkets— oh, no—when I was starting out in sales I uncovered potential leads everywhere I went. If I happened upon any person, place, or thing that somehow related to my line of products, I looked at it as a prospect and I made contact as soon as I got back to work (we didn't yet have the relative luxury of cell phones, or Blackberries, or even computers).

I won't say that my success was spectacular at first, but I know I got many more orders than I would have if I'd been thumbing my way through the magazine stand at the supermarket instead of stalking the aisles like a madman taking down names and contact information off of labels. Was I a workaholic? Some may think so; but to me, I was simply taking every opportunity I could to become a success. It seemed obvious to me that by digging and digging, I would soon be climbing and climbing.

We can't sell our wares if we have no one to sell them to—that's why generating leads, networking, and gaining people's trust so that they will refer you to their colleagues is so crucial in sales. Your clients and customers are your bread and butter and you can expect to spend a lot of time buttering your bread. First, we'll talk more about bringing those precious clients into your fold, and then we'll move on to the musts and the nuances of your presentation and follow-up.

Generating Leads

My very first sales job required very little need for searching for leads; the sales team only did business with clients who called in looking for information or a quote on a particular item. I stayed with that company for two years, but I knew after just a few weeks that it would be a constant uphill battle to meet my goals and make good commissions if my potential leads were so limited.

When I moved on to my next sales job at H.S. Crocker, I immediately asked management about the opportunities that would be available to me as far as drumming up new business. The sky seemed to be the limit. I felt free to make any call to any potentially interested party, or to anyone who could steer me in the right direction. The truth is, I didn't need my manager to tell me where to look for leads—they were all right there in front of me on the shelves of supermarkets and health food stores I visited everywhere (while dear Darla patiently tapped her toe). Labels of all sorts, sizes, and types, as well as the names of the companies who either packed or sold the product were literally at my fingertips. For me, collecting leads was a piece of cake, or on a piece of cake, as the case may be.

Naturally, not all salespeople have a product so easily researched. It wouldn't have stopped me and it shouldn't give you an excuse not to do your homework, either. Every product, even the most obscure, has a market—otherwise the business would fail. If you have difficulty generating leads for companies who need the type of product you sell, there are absolutely other places to look, as well as some creative ways to generate referrals. Trade magazines and trade shows featuring products in your field can be extremely useful, even if you simply reach someone who can help guide you.

For example, if you are in the boomerang business, and you find a listing for Acme Australian Artifacts in a trade magazine, the company may already have an overstock of boomerangs. You may be disappointed by Acme, but if your presentation is strong and your manner enthusiastic, Acme may well give you the contact information for Bill's Boomerangs, whom the manager at Acme knows is in need of dozens of boomerangs. If your presentation, whether it's by phone or in person, is weak, you'll no doubt get a brusque "thank you, we're not interested." If you've honed your skills, though, if you use those Four D's, if you are the embodiment of confident but not pushy, friendly but not falsely so, knowledgeable and curious at the same time, and as formal as the situation calls for but never inappropriate—just polite—you'd be very surprised by the things people will do to help you.

I sat down with my manager almost immediately after being hired and learned as much about the products as my brain and notepads would hold. My manager took me down to the line so I could see for myself how these items were produced. At the risk of sounding like a broken record, you simply must know your product inside and out—every aspect of it. I was very excited—I wanted to know the name of every machine and how it worked; I wanted to be able to give my prospects every detail possible about my products, how they worked and how they were manufactured. What makes them "good" products? What products were in the pipeline? How did this work? Why did that work that way? Never once was anyone bothered by answering my questions.

H.S. Crocker—a company that celebrated 150 years in business in 2006—had a lot to offer me, so much so that I devoted the rest of my career to them. I serve now as the President and CEO. The cooperative relationship that has always been there between sales and management has paid off in more ways than I could ever have imagined. My success has resulted from the manner in which I applied myself, and from what I learned from the company—the ideal situation in sales.

Networking

Clearly, researching leads is essential, but networking can lead you to an endless supply of new leads as well. Most folks realize this, but unfortunately, they put the brakes on out of a lack of confidence or they become discouraged too soon. It's tough for the most gregarious of us to walk into a room full of strangers and start chatting them up. Remember, these folks are here for the same reason you are—to generate business. You also need to recognize that we're all human. There's no shame in introducing yourself to someone. I usually begin with a smile and a simple introduction. Guess what? People love to talk, especially about themselves. There are salespeople out there who have made million dollar deals just because they chose the right person to chat with. Leave the timid side of you at home, put on a big smile, and commit yourself to attending as many industry-related events as possible. If you find yourself freezing up, it might not be a bad idea to take some acting classes at your local community college or theater. Or, you can even stand in front of a mirror and practice. You can break out of shyness—it just takes practice, and, as always, persistence and perseverance. There is a direct correlation to the amount of effort put forth and the eventual success you'll enjoy from it.

Personally, I network with everyone from machine builders to cup suppliers. I attend trade shows, along with any other events associated, even loosely, with my line of sales. Your line of sales may be quite different, but there are always means by which you can explore further growth of your product line. Exploring trade shows is a must and an old standard. Today, the Internet can also be an efficient and all-encompassing way to find prospective contacts. There's no way to overstate it: networking is the single best way to drum up business. Your contacts won't grow overnight, but the more people you can introduce yourself to, the better. The more opportunities you have to look someone in the eye and ask for their business (or for a referral), the better the chance you'll start building an impressive client list. But that's not all—now you also have people out there who are willing to help you out by word-of-mouth, and so on and so on.

There is a proper and an improper way to network. Always remember that the potential client you are speaking with is your first priority. You are not there to try and pick this client's brain for five more new leads; you ought to give your full attention to that particular prospect and to convince him or her to consider buying from you. But toward the end of the conversation, if things have gone well, there is no reason you can't mention that you are open to new clients and if he or she has anyone in mind, to give you a call. Mention it as an aside for now, and close the conversation with a return to this prospect's business. Then, always end off with a very sincere and warm "thank you," accompanied by a handshake and an exchange of business cards. When this prospect becomes a client (because you did such a great job during your initial meeting) and you are more familiar with each other—when they are absolutely sure that they have your full attention, not just in meetings, but throughout the process—you can feel free to open up a bit more and ask them to keep an eye out for you. There is a way to make everyone feel like they are Number One in your book. Always offer to return the favor; soon you can make recommendations and referrals on their behalf as well.

Here are some suggestions to start your "lead tree."

1. Read trade magazines.
2. Research leads in magazines dealing with other aspects of your industry.
3. Attend trade shows aligned with your industry.
4. Ask good customers to refer other clients to you.
5. Contact machine builders that supply your industry.
6. Contact contract packagers that work in your industry.
7. Ask key customers what trade shows benefit them the most and why.
8. Research stores that relate to your industry for leads.
9. When calling prospects, if appropriate, ask if there are other people or businesses they know that may also be looking for assistance.
10. Always be sure to follow up with a thank-you letter.

Referrals

Your referral customers are an ongoing source of good will and advertising—never forget that—and never forget to treat them as such. Your new clients can quickly become a valuable support system because other customers who have benefited from your reliable, creative, and knowledgeable sales representation have already vouched for you. In turn, they spread that information to other potential customers. The process of obtaining referral customers is just like planting seeds. You till the field, plant the seeds, and after that, it's your hard work, dedication, and determination that will reap the benefits.

Your long-term, existing customers can steer you to new prospects, especially if you've proven to them that you have a great track record as regards follow-up, and even more so if they like you. As long as anyone else associated with the account at your company is agreeable to the idea, you might even call the client to ask for guidance or to make recommendations for you. In this often chaotic and impersonal world, we forget that people actually feel good about helping other people, and your customer will be happy to help as long as they aren't helping one of their competitors! As always, be sure to follow up with a thank-you note whether the lead works out or not—you never know what this customer may come up with in the future.

Referrals naturally come as your career in sales grows, too. When a company you represent loses employees, those employees may well transition to other companies. If they want to make an impression on their new employers, recommending you is one way for them to do that. Your relationship with your clients is symbiotic. Your job is to support them, offer knowledge, and provide them with better solutions for purchasing products so they can be recognized for the work they are doing, regardless of whether they stay with a certain company or if they move on. Don't forget! Be sure to call the replacement employee at the first company so that you don't lose their business. You'll find in many cases that making sure all bases are covered is like wooing a potential mate: you must act graciously, quickly, and with astounding politeness.

The greatest feeling in the world is having a referral call you. It means that you have provided excellent service to other customers, and as a result, you are making headway, you are gaining ground, you are seeing your efforts pay off, and you are growing. Every customer referral you receive means that you have made a good impression on someone. I try to make sure that every prospect I call on, whether I get the business or not, will remember my presentation and follow-up efforts. I've found that sometimes the buyer may call just to keep his current supplier honest, but that doesn't matter. The main thing is that he or she called you, and that in itself may open up some new doors for you.

Prospecting

Prospecting takes time, but the dedication of your time is the most important thing you have to offer. It's not surprising that the word "prospecting" applies both to searching for job leads and for precious metals. You may have to dig through a lot of muck first, but it's all in the effort to strike gold! Prospecting takes time, but that's what you personally have to sell: your time.

When you sit behind your desk and think, "My goodness, what happens now?" the answer is to pursue prospects and referrals— making calls and setting up appointments so that your time is not wasted. Search the Internet. Read about your market and research where to find leads. Are your prospects doing business with companies other than yours? Of course they are! But they are always looking for a better product, and not always at a lower price. Better performance brings better plant-operation efficiency, and if you're lucky, you may be able to assist in the cost area as well. You may have a more efficient delivery system, you may have more options…or perhaps they'll just like you better and make a change.

What if you are selling a product where leads are not so simply found? First of all, remember that there is a market for your product out there or your business would fail. Remember that there will always be some kind of organization, or newsletter, or, again, a trade magazine, that has been created for your line, usually for people just like you who want to network. Shows geared to your product lines and individuals that can direct you to the right place are out there if you just ask. If you don't ask, you'll never know. Constant digging and asking questions can go a long way, as long as you don't come off as rude or pushy. The person on the other end of the line in this situation is the one in power. They can decide whether you are worth helping by your language and attitude. If you can learn to prospect well, there is nothing to stop you from being a great success. Can you dig it?

CHAPTER SEVEN

Closing the Deal and Following Up

The First Meeting with the Prospect

We've discussed ways you can perform valuable investigative work when trying to acquire a new account. The critical point is that your effort will give you an edge on your competitors, even if they, too, are attempting to woo the prospect. Most new clients change vendors when they are dissatisfied with their current supplier. There may not be any problems with the client's production lines, but you need to know that first so you're clear about where to funnel your energy and salesmanship.

Usually a prospect becomes willing to talk to you if they want to know more about your product, if they want to see whether your product is more economical than the one they're already using, or if they have become dissatisfied with your competition. However you get in the door, it's up to you to show what you and your product can do and how well it will perform—and that means homework. Don't go to a potential customer unprepared; be ready to shine, address his or her current concerns, and talk about how your product will serve them better.

If you received a call from a prospect who is unhappy with his current supplier, ask the right questions so you are prepared when you meet. This is especially important if you were called because that buyer is reaching out for help. Now is the time for you to do what is expected of you. Don't go in thinking it's a slam dunk; nothing in this world is that easy. Recognize it as a golden opportunity, go in with your best foot forward, and be ready to ask questions and then set a date for a return visit.

On the other hand, if you are the party trying to convince a company to change suppliers, you must go in with a very convincing attitude. Present your product, describe its benefits, and make it clear why and how you and your company feel it can improve the way the prospect does business. Always remember you are not there to put your competitor down. Rather, acknowledge that the competitor has a good product, but you feel yours is better. If your product can reduce lost time on the production line or solve other problems, its cost is well worth the time and money saved. Remember to ask if you can talk to the people who work on the line; mention that since these workers are the people who know the machines best, they can offer information with regard to any problems that need to be corrected. When you speak with the workers on the production line, tell them that you are truly interested in making their jobs easier, and that you want your product to improve line efficiency. They will tell you what they need and what will help them. Their management team will usually agree, as they know that these are the people who make or break the company.

Here's a typical example of a professional, informational, and personable sales visit:

"Mr. Client, I thought you'd be interested in this particular label because it works in a unique way. We've perfected a method in which two labels become one, and when used at the store level, the clerk pulls apart one piece of the label, leaving the other intact. This kind of label provides verification and an actual receipt that allows you to track each of these particular products sold."

Then, let the client pull apart the two-piece label and experiment. About the time you're ready to finish up the meeting, casually mention, "You might like to take a look at our catalog of products."

Whether the client considers it or not, you are demonstrating that you do, in fact, have other products to offer. You want the client to begin brainstorming about how perhaps several of your company's products can be useful to him. It also shows the client that your product base is always evolving; even if they are not interested in what you have to offer them now, that doesn't mean in two months you won't have something new that they will indeed want. I have been in countless meetings, somehow doubting that the client was interested in a certain product. But as I thumbed through my sample book showing the various products I had to offer, I've been amazed by how often a seemingly disinterested client would say, "Hold on a minute. That looks interesting. Let me call in Mr. or Mrs. So and So to take a look. They may want more information." Now you've got your toe in the door, even though it wasn't in the way you expected.

You'll be able to gauge your prospect's attitude fairly quickly. At the appropriate moment, begin to explore what is more important to him, cost or plant efficiency? More than likely, both will be important. Ask the client for detailed information about his plant and equipment: What is the line speed? Are there currently any problems? Where would they like to see greater output? The more information you get, the more clarity you will have about the solutions you can offer. You will be asked for a rough price estimate and timeline. An excellent response would be:

"I am willing to review the process and make suggestions at my expense. If you are not satisfied, then neither of us has lost. But I will be able to show you how to save, not only in price, but in material choice."

When reviewing the client's production process, you will garner a wealth of knowledge by talking to engineers and line operators— ideally, you ought to know how the competitors' product arrives as well. Your knowledge of this information, coupled with outlining the alternative approaches your company will provide, will prove your commitment to the client and his or her company.

Additionally, during this process of selling yourself to the client, offer them only one item at first. Don't be greedy and ask for all the business. When you show respect for your competitor, you are communicating to the buyer that you merely want a chance to prove yourself and your company, and that their satisfaction, whether it be with your product or the competitor's, is your ultimate goal. Tell the buyer that one small item is acceptable, and that you and your company are prepared to offer the same level of service, price, and quality with one item that you would if you had all the items.

This approach works. Just this past week, a prospect called and needed some help. The prospect wanted a certain type of lid for one of his products; he was happy with the lid itself, but unhappy with certain aspects of its performance. The challenge at that moment was for me to prove to the client that our product was better. As we discussed the problem, I mentioned to him that our adhesives have an ingredient called "Stabilizer 5" which effectively secures a sealed product, but is easy for the consumer to use, thereby addressing the prospect's main concerns. The prospect was intrigued by the "Stabilizer 5" solution. Did I push the envelope a little? Probably, but since I was able to offer him a great solution to the adhesive problem, it really wasn't critical what method I used to get the message across. Sometimes a little frosting on the cake tastes better than a lot of frosting at the risk of being sick. In other words, a little goes a long way.

Follow-Up

Without question, follow-up should always be considered a critical element in your sales strategy. When following up, take your message all the way: outline a hypothetical situation for the prospect that demonstrates how his or her plant efficiency will increase because downtime will decrease and that you can prove it if given the chance.

That's if the prospect has shown some interest, and that's admittedly optimistic advice. Follow-up can be the hardest and most frustrating aspect of your business, too. You made a great presentation, but now you must follow up and wait and follow up and wait and follow up and wait again. Perhaps a voicemail or e-mail to your prospect generates no response. That doesn't make it easy, but no one said it would be; after all, you're trying to convince the prospect that what you're selling is better than what he already has, even if it costs more, sometimes.

Your repeated follow-up efforts are not a waste of time; rather, they're a damn good way to increase your opportunities, I like to think. My follow-up "tickler file" not only reminds me of which regular customers I need to call, but it also jogs memories of any additional prospects, complete with side bars regarding their likes, dislikes, and family information, such as their children's sports activities. People don't usually mind when you ask certain types of personal questions, as long as you keep it simple, professional, and completely aboveboard. Clients are individuals who have risen to their posts for a reason, but no one is above receiving compliments and praise. Have they all seen and heard everything? Probably not, but treat each client as if he has. Your job is to expand a client's base of knowledge by explaining how your company works with customers, the financial benefits of working with your company, and what you can do to make the client's job easier.

When following up with a prospect, be polite. A good approach is, "I just wanted to keep in touch. Let me know if there is anything I can do to help you...and oh, by the way, did I tell you about our new product or idea?" It could be equipment, a product promotion, or a good idea for redesigning his or her product. Be creative and, above all, enthusiastic about the product you're selling so that you pique the interest of the buyer. Have samples available so the client can see and touch them. Let the prospect know how the samples were produced and how they can best be used. Always remember: Knowledge equals power.

Closing the Deal

Many salespeople work very hard to get an order, but can't for the life of them close a deal. From my own observation, it seems that they just continue on conversing instead of simply asking for the purchase order. I guess some people believe that key moment should be one of relaxation, a sigh now that the presentation is over, a smile, and a stare. No! It takes just as much eagerness and determination to ask for the order as it took to get into that prospect's office. Don't be shy! Get the order! Is it easier to just let it slide and hope that the purchase order will be mailed? Sure, but there's a saying I've heard about one bird in the hand...usually that means it's not going to happen.

You need to be prepared to ask for the order, especially after you have done your research, spent time with the prospect, and received a favorable response. You don't have to bombard or annoy them to the point of vexation; instead, in the same confident, knowledgeable, honest manner you presented yourself throughout the meeting, ask the customer if there is any more information he or she needs.

Then segue into asking if you can pick up the purchase order before you leave so that everyone can move forward. If a buyer responds by saying, "Let me get back to you," then ask him what other information he might need. Answer those questions so that you have satisfied the buyer's concerns. If you are told that someone else must approve the purchase order, then ask if both of you can go see that person so the wheels can begin turning. Carry the conversation as though the customer doesn't seem ready to bite because you haven't provided them with all the information they need. This is when, more than ever, it is crucial to have complete faith in yourself and your product.

Not all situations play out like this. There are many times when you negotiate a deal and ask for and receive the order immediately after you both have agreed on the terms. The main thing in all of this is that you ask for the order. Don't be afraid of what you have to do or think about all the effort you have put in getting to this point. Don't let this opportunity pass you by! Have enough respect for your own work and effort and accomplish your goal of getting the order and closing the deal. I cannot overstate the reality that you can't get the deal if you don't ask for it.

Will there be times when there are delays? There certainly will, and even though you may have to wait a little longer, don't lose sight of making this simple request: "When can I get the purchase order?" Sometimes you may need to ask the buyer a question that will force his hand, so to speak. For example, ask if he can forward you the artwork so you can get the proofs out to him and get started. Either way, you are moving forward in a positive manner, and you are being supportive of your customer at the same time.

One more thing: Taking a customer for granted is not only bad business, it's also rude. The customer assumes that you will follow through and make sure that their order, whether large or small, is handled like a brick of gold. Each customer feels that their order should be considered just as important as anyone else's. Not all orders will be large, but you must treat that client as if he were a king. Today, that client may be operating on a small scale, but who knows what will happen in the future. Certain loyal customers, however, deserve your special attention. You have to do whatever it takes to care for your customer and keep them coming back to you.

You Got the Deal!

Sales is really comprised of a series of actions that (hopefully) will be ongoing. When you close a deal, there are things that must be followed up and checked on a daily basis to be sure that they are being completed exactly as promised to your customer. You may have a team that does all this for you, but who is ultimately responsible for the order getting to the customer on time and looking fantastic? That's you. There is valid logic behind the saying "If you want something done, do it yourself." Obviously, if you work on a large scale, you cannot be a one-man show, so it is imperative that you trust the people you delegate these tasks to.

As you get into your work day, keep communications wide open— never shut yourself off. What you are doing is making sure that you, your company, the people making your product, and your clients are all kept abreast of what's going on. If a change is needed, then you can call your customer before the problem becomes a crisis. It can be a little problem or a larger one, but by letting the customer know, they can give their input, or you may arrive at a compromise. Everyone, from the CEO to the machinists on the line, and ultimately the client, will appreciate the fact that they can rely on you and you can rely on them. You are a team and the working environment isn't frenetic and uncomfortable. You are creating an atmosphere all around that encourages trust, that engenders a calm and efficient process from start to finish, and that leaves you looking pretty and feeling good.

What's best for everybody? Your system, your input, and your effort. Do you have the time for this? Yes, you do—as long as you are organized. If you are truly organized, you can accomplish a host of things on a daily basis. You need to have an organizational system, a plan, a method by which to accomplish your goals—and it must be in writing. At the end of each day, jot down the things that must be done the next day. You may miss a few items, but overall your list will cover the vast majority of them. When you begin work the following morning, start with your follow-up calls before anything else. I cannot stress enough the importance of working the phone and answering e-mails as soon as you get to your desk. As the day progresses, other matters, some more pressing than others, will come up, and you will need to address everything in a truly organized manner. I use my particular method of information-packed index cards, along with other ways to keep what's in front of me tidy. I never want to be smothered by things I put off simply because I didn't feel like doing them; you may have a different way of organizing yourself and your day.

Don't work from memory alone because you may miss something—it can lead to mistakes you can't afford to make.

CHAPTER EIGHT

. . . .

Playing Nicely in the Sandbox

Team Play

Regardless of whether you're a salesperson or a manager, you need to be able to work efficiently and successfully with your clients and prospects. But you also need to work expeditiously and cooperatively with all of the people in your office, including assistants, line workers, research and development folks, janitorial staff, you name it—you must have a team mentality to achieve maximum results for everyone, including yourself. Maneuvering office politics can be challenging, but because your full engagement in the job at hand means you are always in the trenches working with others, it is critical to establish and maintain positive relationships with both your clients and your co-workers.

For me, as CEO of my company, "working in the trenches" refers to being involved—hands on—in the daily activity of working with customers, but that's not all. My sales force works with prospects and customers on a daily basis, but they must also work with everyone else who plays a part in creating, producing, and delivering the product to the client, just as I have during my entire career. As a manager, to give input to a sales team without actually handling accounts myself is wrong as far as I'm concerned. Many managers feel their role is simply to guide their sales force and assist on calls. While I feel there's nothing wrong with that, when I'm handling several accounts myself, I'm also in touch with what my sales team (and everyone else involved) is doing on a daily basis.

Perhaps other managers think this micro-management approach takes away from handling their own responsibilities, but when you think about it, managers have their hand in sales every day whether they realize it or not. All managers have their own styles; I prefer not only assisting my sales force, but also handling my own sales accounts as well. There have been many times when I've conducted research and development testing at a customer's plant, either alone or with my salespeople and R&D director, because I want to be aware of, and involved in, every step along the way. One might assume that this method usurps the salesperson's authority, but I disagree. I find, instead, that my involvement breeds confidence in my salespeople, and I believe it's even more impressive to my customers, especially when I can assure them that they're in very good hands with their rep.

In sales, you need to ask the appropriate people in your company to be involved as well. As a salesperson, if you ask your manager for support, you will most likely receive it. But when asking for support, be prepared to present what you are going to do and how you plan to approach a particular situation. Your manager wants, deserves, and NEEDS all of this information and you are being given the opportunity to show what you're willing to do to perform your job like an ace. Likewise, you should expect your management team to be there for you. This not only provides you with the support you need, but it gives management the opportunity to see you in action so they can evaluate your professional skills.

Keeping Customers in the Loop

Both your company and your accounts need to be kept updated about what's going on, and consistent follow-up is the way to achieve this; if a change is needed, call your customer before the problem becomes a crisis and they will appreciate your direct approach. Whether the problem is small or large, let the customer know what's going on. You need their input, and you may be able to decide on a workable compromise—for example, they may accept a partial shipment, or decide to delay a shipment altogether.

Decisions like this can only be made if the customer knows what's going on, and especially when he or she hears the possible solutions to any given problem. Never assume that a customer will take for granted that an order could be late. In fact, assume the opposite: the customer expects that you will follow through on the promised arrival date, and that you will handle their order, large or small, as if it were a Fabergé egg. Each customer feels that his order is just as important as that of the guy with a larger order. Treat each customer with the same respect, and never, under any circumstances, make a customer feel as if he doesn't count. Everybody counts, and they all have equal value and deserve equal consideration. Don't ever underestimate a customer; they may be small today, but tomorrow they could be a Fortune 500 company, and a customer will always remember how you treated them.

Troubleshooting: At Least I Can Laugh About It Now!

Find me a salesperson who doesn't have a collection of stories of mishaps and misadventures and I will show you a salesperson who isn't doing their job. In sales, you are confronted constantly with situations in which creative thinking on your feet is necessary. Sometimes your creative solutions are meant to help out your client; sometimes it's just to save your own sanity. I remember times when I have had soda spilled all over my dress shirt and sport coat just as I walked into the customer's office; how about the many occasions when the airport has lost my luggage? Then there's the inevitable delayed flight due to weather, yet when you call in to your office, there's not a cloud in the sky. Just when you think you have heard, seen, smelled, witnessed, dreamed, or thought of all the possible mishaps, something else is bound to happen and reset the bar yet again.

There are a myriad of irritating, infuriating, nauseating, uncomfortable, and all-out catastrophic things that can happen to us as we travel the many highways and byways of sales. In most cases, all we can do is laugh about it once the bizarre disaster has passed because in the end you made it through in one piece (and what's more, you closed the deal!). There will be at least one time (if not several) when everything you have promised to your customer and have confirmed with your plant will evaporate before your eyes. You cannot crawl in a hole and die; you must bounce back and make a positive recovery. It takes a lot of determination and a method by which you can take control and stand tall again. You must make sure the instructions you gave are understood and acknowledged, and then you must explain to your customer that you will correct the problem and that you stand behind your word 100%. Follow up with a letter and an e-mail assuring all involved parties that you will stop at nothing to make sure the problem is rectified. You also have to make sure that your plant knows how important it is to make a smooth recovery so that your customers will know that you mean business. Don't be afraid to stand up and be counted. If others around you think you are crazy or tap-dancing in place, that's fine. In the long haul, the plant employees and the customers will respect what you are doing because it's the right thing to do!

When you have invested your life in sales, there will be circumstances where you'll feel looked down upon, treated as an irritant, or just plain disliked. In my experience, I've found that people who treat others badly are usually just jealous, for whatever reason. The chilly vibes could be from a vendor or a supplier who thinks that you are putting too much pressure on them to lower their prices, only because you are seeking a better program that will eventually help your company stay more competitive. In these types of situations, I always stay focused on one thing: my goal is to help my company. Just because others don't like my ideas doesn't make them wrong. A vendor once told me that I was a tough negotiator, but he also understood that I was only doing what was expected of me and nothing less.

Salespeople really need to have fairly thick skin—you must deal with frequent rejection, and then once you've got a client roster, you'll have to deal with customers, co-workers, suppliers, and even your own manager (or your own sales force if you are the manager), and even the best of us run into problems, both small and large. We are all human and sometimes we let personal feelings get in the way of good decision making. I've made a lot of difficult decisions over the years, both as a salesman and as a manager, and at no time did I ever feel that what I was fighting for wasn't worth it.

Just because you disagree with someone, please try never to hold a grudge—you will be doing yourself a weighty disservice. I have certainly had disagreements with members of my sales team, or with a client, but sooner rather than later, it's best to simply move on and put any bad feelings to rest. Time spent grumbling and obsessing over your personal feelings is time, energy, and money wasted. I'm sure there are suppliers out there who feel like they have to dodge bullets when meeting with me. Maybe they're right, but what's more important is that they perform with the same high standards that I have promised my customers.

Handling Difficult Clients

Is there a time you should just let go and have an account reassigned to someone else? Perhaps, but then again, isn't this just the easy way out? Who ever said that every account would go down as easily as a hot buttered scone? Do you sometimes want to tell that buyer to take a flying leap? Of course—but all that you have accomplished then is satisfying your ego while damaging the reputation of your company. Will there be a company that should be asked to take their business elsewhere? Absolutely. But before you do that, talk to your manager, see what his or her thoughts are, and come to a sound solution together. Perhaps you'll both decide that this account has caused too many problems, or that the customer's expectations versus the profit made on the account does not justify making others customers orders late when they are at the same profit level but are more willing to work with you and not against you.

When you run into difficult clients, ask your manager for support and you will more than likely receive it. Beforehand, be sure to have several possible solutions to share yourself. How would you plan to approach the situation? Expect your management team to be there for you and in return, if they are true blue, they will also have the opportunity to see you in action and what your professional approach to a prospect or customer might be.

What I have talked about so far is not rocket science; rather, these ideas are sound, honest, and dependable ways to act professionally when presenting to a buyer. Will there be a buyer who is difficult to deal with? Of course, and he won't be the only one you encounter—you can count on that. But you will quickly learn to see the difference between professional buyers, and buyers who are only trying to get the lowest price they can with no attention to quality of the product or the service received. Believe me; the trouble you will encounter in the future with unprofessional buyers isn't worth the effort you expend trying to convince them to go with your company.

Working with difficult clients does, in fact, have its place in the world of sales. These clients challenge you to be better prepared and better equipped to demonstrate your product and the benefits of working with your company. In some cases, you will have to establish a relationship when a company has brought in a new buyer; in other cases, you will be working with potential customers or prospects who need input from you. In either case, you must call upon all of your personal talents, knowledge, and skills to work successfully with companies who need more "babysitting." Don't let the challenges throw you off course; instead, see them as opportunities to enhance and hone your skills as a salesperson, and remember that facing each challenge instead of trying to hide only builds your repertoire of sales techniques.

Prospect Challenges, Part II

There have to be ground rules in any avenue of sales and some are easier to follow than others. There will certainly be success stories where you have bent over backwards to help a client, and that becomes the turning point that establishes and cements a working relationship that benefits everyone involved. But there are clients with whom it seems you can never win no matter how hard you try. Will you win all the battles? Absolutely not! But you owe it to yourself to give it all you've got even if it just turns out to be a learning experience.

One definition of the "difficult" client is the one who just won't give you an answer. This situation shouldn't give you an excuse to blow them off in the same manner. Dealing with this sort of difficult client demands patience, patience, and more patience. Along the way, though, through voicemail, e-mail, and letters sent by post, you can still promote your product, refer to other available products, and mention new products to come. Price is always a definite factor, so ask, "How much of a savings would you expect if you changed suppliers?" Of course the prospect's response might be an unrealistic number, but let the prospect know, "I may not be able to reach that number without more information," or "In viewing your operations, I'm not certain I can reach that number, but I am willing to try." Even if the savings the prospect wants is completely unrealistic, at least you've let him or her know it may be possible, and you may just get a return phone call. The point is: it ain't over 'til it's over.

Let's compare the professional buyer with the difficult, unprofessional buyer. The professional buyer will be tough, armed with details, and will make it clear that his or her company requires a certain cost savings for them to even consider working with you. The other side of the coin is the buyer who negotiates a deal with you, then wants to renegotiate every time another vendor knocks on his door. No matter how painful it may be, you must first explain your cost structure, and then all of the benefits and services you are including for free. Will he challenge you? Of course, with the response that the other vendor offers the same service, perhaps even at a lower cost.

Here's an example: Imagine that you are selling a foil lid to a yogurt company. Your product has finally been chosen for testing because you have called upon this prospect for three years, and during that time, you have kept in touch with the plant superintendent and the head of maintenance. By keeping in touch with these individuals, you have learned that they have an over-sealing problem with their current lid: the rim of the cup melts when the foil lid is applied and sealed with heat. Consequently, the over cap doesn't fit correctly, the foil is imbedded in the plastic rim, and this creates a weld or causes the foil to tear when the consumer removes it from the cup. This problem is obviously unacceptable to everyone, particularly the ultimate consumer, who has now spilled cherry yogurt on her white cashmere sweater and will never buy that brand of yogurt again.

Finally you get your chance: the company begins testing your lid product. After several tests, however, the head engineer at the corporate office decides the new lid material is not strong enough; moreover, they have decided to change their eight-ounce cup and do away with the plastic over cap. In addition, you find out that they are currently talking with a supplier across the border who's pitching that their material is significantly better. Just when you thought you were in the home stretch, you are stopped dead in your tracks. Is it time to give up? Absolutely not! Instead, you persevere: talk with the buyer about what your product can do and compare the differences between your product and your competitor's. Never take a defensive or aggressive tone—maintain your professionalism at all times. Keep the dialogue going, like two people chatting.

Now it's time to roll up your sleeves and prepare to demonstrate that your product is, in fact, better, and you can prove it. Do your home-work from top to bottom. Look at every part of the process your prospective customer uses. In this case, for example, you want to look at his machine performance and maintenance, the cup rim, the foil lid, and the quality of your own lid. You want test results showing easy peel, high burst strength, and good puncture resistance. Then look at the whole process of machine output and demonstrate how you can meet or exceed the shift standards for plant performance.

If your prospect still does not accept your offer, then offer him another option: you'll produce your lid for one of their plants while the competitor continues their work at the same plant. Here's the key, though—ask to work with the plant this company is having the most difficulty with. Present this offer with the utmost class and professionalism, and make sure your data is so extensive, your final presentation is sure to exceed that of the competition. Any good businessperson knows that cost is not always the most critical factor. Once your testing is completed, you'll find yourself ahead of the game in quality, performance, and professionalism.

In today's world of change, technology, and almost immediate communication, you must always remember that there is one very important element that matters more than anything: you, the person. You, the dedicated, determined, desirous, and enthusiastic individual. This is what prospects will truly respond to, and what will ultimately lead to your success. When you are willing to go to great effort because you believe in your product so very much, the buyer needs to ask himself, "What's this guy got that has him so excited, so enthusiastic, so willing to go so far to prove it to me?" Your personality, along with the actions you're willing to put time into on his or her behalf, is guaranteed to breed interest, at the very least.

The Personal Factor: Recognizing Personality Differences

I've mentioned the art of "reading" someone several times. It's a salesperson's great fortune to learn this talent, for you'll always be two steps ahead of the game. The buyer/salesperson relationship actually is something of a game, like walking through a flea market ready to take part in that great ritual we call "getting a deal." When you can observe the tiniest of details about the person you are negotiating with, you can begin to learn things that might be very useful. Does your buyer have a shelf full of baseball memorabilia or old movie posters on the wall? Does he or she look you in the eye or maniacally shuffle papers when you are talking? Is he a joke-a-minute guy or is she a very well-groomed woman? Always make it a priority to observe and then present the "you" that fits the situation best.

There are as many types of buyers as there are types of people, and that's part of what makes our jobs all the more challenging. One of your roles as a salesperson is to adapt to each buyer's individual personality. You must be like a chameleon. Remember, you're not changing the manner in which you treat each buyer's particular quirks, you are working within the guidelines that buyer offers you. What you are aiming for is to use your personality—to sell yourself—so that those guidelines can match up with your guidelines.

Never lose a buyer's respect, as respect is a universal element necessary for anybody you deal with or approach. You may hang up the phone and utter a few four letter words, but never, ever lose control of your manners when you're with a client. It can be difficult sometimes, but you cannot ever behave as if you're better or more learned than anyone else, especially a client or a coworker. As the old saying goes, until you have walked in another man's moccasins, you have no business being opinionated or disrespectful.

Yes, you will encounter buyers you wish you had never met, but you must set aside your personal feelings or you will fail. And when you do finally sign that new customer, it will be all the more satisfying. There is sound reason for the notion that "the customer is always right," because as a seller it is necessary for you to meet the customer's needs no matter what your emotional investment may be. Even if a client is particularly difficult to deal with, they are responsible for your financial livelihood and you must ensure the sale, for your own benefit. If the customer really is so terribly difficult to handle, it's just all the more reason for you to meet all of his needs efficiently so that your contact is limited—they have nothing to complain about! If you perform well, even if you don't personally like the client, he or she may well bring more business your way in the future. There is never a reason to burn bridges; always remain professional and you will be rewarded.

Mixing Business and Friendship

Some folks shy away from mixing friendship with business. I just can't seem to understand how developing an amiable relationship with anyone you work with could be problematic, as long as both parties are mature enough to recognize what is appropriate for friends to do for each other versus what colleagues can do for each other. No one gets preferential treatment from me because I treat all of my customers with the same honesty, politesse, and cooperation. Some of my customers become my friends because we enjoy each other's company. That doesn't mean that I'll bump another customer's job to the back of the line just to help out a pal. We all understand that nothing comes before good, honest professionalism.

So whether you are invited to call on a prospect by the prospect themselves or if you have been "allowed" in to make a presentation, step into the meeting with the intention of finding both a new customer and a new friend. Most companies look for team effort and this is no different; you must employ your best strategy toward making everyone feel comfortable, let everyone know that you can take control and get the job done within a timeline acceptable to your prospect. Smile, offer an appropriate compliment, and stay loose but professional. Above all, make sure you all walk away with a clear understanding of what is needed next and what expectations you all have of each other. Your demeanor alone will help convince them that you are the person they can count on, just as they would count on a friend.

There have been many times when a vendor or customer has invited me out for lunch or dinner. A meeting over a meal or cocktails can loosen everyone up; sometimes jokes are shared, or personal stories, and a very conducive atmosphere is created for making friends. Usually, I will accept the invitation; sometimes, considering my current job position, I must decline as I have too much work yet to be completed on my desk. My modus operandi with customers on the first meeting is to be friendly, but not so friendly as to display the wrong impression: a "slick" salesman who will tell the customer anything they want to hear whether it's actually feasible or not. I would rather a vendor or supplier spend their time and energy giving me the best product they can as opposed to taking me to a ritzy restaurant. I truly appreciate the offer, but I must always put my company and the customers we serve first. As a salesperson, you will frequently find yourself in situations where a customer becomes more than a customer—he or she becomes a real friend. That's fine, just as long as you can both maintain an objective and subjective stance when a problem arises, putting you in the position of having to defend your company and likely losing both the account and the friendship.

On the other hand, everyone should remember never to sell friendships short. You can be a friend as well as a good salesperson and still be a boss while you're at it. No one ever promised that life would be fair, but it sure helps when folks realize that you can always be a friend as well as a professional. When you keep this in the back of your mind, your various dealings and conversations are almost guaranteed to go more smoothly, with both parties embracing compromise and the main goal—keeping existing clients happy and bringing new clients on every day—a cooperative exercise.

How you retain your friendship when problems arise is like walking a tightrope—you don't want to lose a client or a friend—and this advice applies to all customers, not just the ones you like socially. My advice begins with cooling your jets for a few minutes. Don't let emotion take control over common sense. Then, you must examine the facts to see where the fault really lies; is it with your company or with the customer? After you establish the problem area you must present your side to your customer in such a way that they understand what has happened and how it needs to be corrected. When it comes time to discuss the problem with your client, don't come on strong. Instead, continue to maintain a friendly tone and present the problem in such a way that he or she understands, focusing mainly on how you and your co-workers arrived at the final conclusion. If part of the problem is yours, absolutely stand up and accept responsibility. No one will ever fault you for being honest. If it turns out to be the customer's fault, then make sure your customer understands, but doesn't feel the need to be defensive. After all, mistakes happen. If the responsibility lies in both camps, then step right up and accept that part for which you are responsible, again, without ever becoming defensive.

Regardless of where the mistake occurred, after you have reached a conclusion, a plan of action must be agreed upon right away. For example, if the fault lies with your company and credits are needed, they should be issued immediately or as promptly as possible. If, on the other hand, the problem began with the customer, they should advise their accounting department to process an invoice for payment. You may even be asked by the customer to work out an amortization schedule. If so, then check with your boss and strongly suggest that you make the deal. It not only helps you, it helps the reputation of your company. After all, we are all looking for ways to make problems go away with the best possible solution for all concerned. If you can be both a friend and a truly talented salesperson, your customer will never forget your effort and assertiveness in resolving the problem.

Ducking Responsibility

Believe it—not many days will go by without your finding yourself in a real quandary. You process an order for a customer and feel you have done your best: the job goes fine, you meet the dates requested, and deliver the order ahead of schedule. Then, some kind of problem occurs and you suddenly find yourself in a pickle. Now your plant has to scurry to get a replacement order out within seven days so the customer's operations don't shut down, and you must immediately request that credits be issued for the original defective materials. In this case, you are not guilty of ducking your responsibility—either to your customer or to your own plant—because you have kept everyone informed of the problem and you have worked to reach a solution.

About eight weeks go by, and now your customer claims that he had more losses than originally reported. Your plant has already handled the credits with their vendor and issued credits to the customer. Where do you go from here? You can hide, but you can't run! There is a time and a place for issues to be resolved, and to the best of your knowledge, that has already happened. Is it appropriate for the customer to come back eight weeks later and report additional losses? Certainly not! Your plant jumped through hoops to rerun the order, and went into overtime and double time so that your customer had the product in as timely a fashion as possible. How can you now be expected to issue credits for an additional amount of money to the customer? This is not an easy situation, and it's one that will require you to demonstrate strength, wisdom, and common sense.

First, you'll need to sit down with the customer and go over everything that has happened with this order. Acknowledge that your company was responsible for the problem, but also that your company solved the problem. Explain what you and your company did to keep them going—you reacted immediately to resolve the problem, moved other customers out of the schedule, worked on a weekend to get the order sent air (at your expense) to keep his operations running, and above all, you put his needs first. Then ask the customer to think about what would be fair for both parties, given what your company did.

These situations are never easy and often demand restraint on your part, along with understanding and empathy for your customer's predicament. Stay focused and above all, do not lose your composure; instead, listen to his points and then make your points. When he speaks, take notes so that when you respond you will address them in chronological order. In the end, there will always be a compromise; yes, you may have to work out another credit, a reduction in price on the next order, or perhaps no freight charges for a period of time.

Sometimes, you've just got to be as creative as you can. I remember a time when we were running significantly behind in our delivery of a product to a customer. We had the order in the house and ready to print and the initial delivery date was four weeks. As things turned out, however, we weren't ready to ship and the four weeks would become six weeks, because we had to ship to the West coast. Coming up with something to appease the customer was of the utmost importance. It was "do or die" by that time. When the customer called, it was wintertime in Chicago and everything was frozen over, which gave me an idea. While talking on the phone to the customer, I mentioned that my story of what had happened was going to be, "while the truck was going through the Rockies in the dead of winter, the truck turned over—but thank God the driver was okay!" For a moment there was total silence. Then the customer commented on what a great story that would have been. There was a pause and you could feel the smile and then hear the laughter. The customer gave me points for creativity, but asked how I could just help him with the situation. Not only did we "replace" the lost order, but we got it to him in record time. I was initially hesitant to include this story but the truth is, sometimes you've just got to do what you've got to do to save everyone's sanity.

The good news is that almost anyone will agree to some kind of compromise. In fact, in today's world, everything is a compromise and everyone must be willing to bend a little bit. Without compromise, none of us would do very well, whether we're talking about our professional lives or our personal lives. So, when faced with a quandary in your professional life, don't duck responsibility, and don't let yourself get caught up in personal reasons for not doing your best in your professional realm. Always accept responsibility for what is appropriate, work toward compromises and solutions, and in the end, you will have better relationships with your customers than you ever thought possible. If all else fails, make sure everyone knows the truck turned over, but the driver's okay!

The Trip from Hell

Things don't always go smoothly. We all have days we wish we could start over again from the beginning. But even after the most trying of experiences—and usually after a few days have passed—you'll find that there is a lesson to be learned (and sometimes even a laugh to be had), regardless of the discomfort and frustration of a day ruled by Murphy's Law.

I'd been calling on one account for two years trying to sell the manufacturer the large, printed circles that are packaged on top of frozen pizzas, often badgering our own plant to get the costs down. Generally, it's acceptable to challenge your manufacturing facility, since they must perform well to help you perform well. You may speak directly with the appropriate people at the facility, or go through your immediate supervisor.

I finally got my first test run of the product, but unbeknownst to me, our plant had transposed the ingredients on the two labels, one sausage and the other, Canadian bacon. When I arrived at the customer's plant with the labels, all production stopped because of the label problem. Needless to say, I went home with my tail between my legs after ten thousand apologies. I kept up communication with the customer, however, and got a second chance. Was it luck? Perhaps, but it was also determination.

For the second test run with the customer, I flew on a commercial airline to Kansas City, then on a twin-engine plane to a small town. When I exited the plane and walked out of the tiny terminal, an elderly gentleman sprinkling the lawn turned to look at a friend driving by, and sprayed my pants with water. I was wearing a wool suit in eighty-five degree weather, and now my pants were soaked. I looked and smelled like a wet sheepdog.

The test run with the customer, however, went very well. When I headed back to the terminal and boarded the small plane, I was asked to sit in the last seat since they needed to "balance the load." During the flight, the co-pilot asked if I would reach under the seat to retrieve a basket of candy and pass it forward, which I did as well as a trained cabin attendant. Besides the soaked wool pants, whose scent I might call "eau de doggy," my "balancing act," and the tricky basket of candy maneuver in the two-engine plane, it just so happened that when I changed planes in Kansas City, we encountered very severe turbulence during the flight. The cabin attendant opened a can of 7-UP on an angle, which naturally sprayed all over my suit, and the cuff of my suit jacket fell directly into my heavily frosted chocolate cake. When I arrived home, my wife opened the door and looked at me in amazement. Long trip? Sure. Tough day? You bet. Would I do it all over again? In a minute. Did I give up selling after all that? Not on your life! I was so high from the success of the test run that nothing could faze me.

On another occasion, early one winter morning, I was to travel by car from Chicago to Wisconsin. I started out on the trip at 6:00 a.m. in the snowy, bitter cold and asked myself, "Do I really want to make this trip, or should I just go to the office, reschedule the appointment, and line up more prospects to see in the future?" As I bounced back and forth with my options, I continued on the interstate toward Wisconsin and the rural area I would be visiting. I told myself that I'd gone this far, so why not just go ahead instead of turning back? It meant not giving up and taking the easy way out, so I continued. It was a mighty good decision.

That day, for some reason unbeknownst to me, several doors to prospects I had been calling on magically opened for me. I had called these folks on a regular basis trying to get appointments for some time; when I finally did schedule a date, not much would progress, but at least I was demonstrating how serious I was and how much I wanted their business. I wasn't expecting much, but that didn't bother me because I operated on the premise that no effort goes unnoticed. Lo and behold, my luck changed on that snowy, bitter day. When I met with my first prospect, he admitted that he was having trouble with his supplier. This was just what I had been waiting for—the opportunity to show off my company and its products. Finally, my persistence and enthusiasm for my product had paid off.

The second prospect I saw that day wasn't experiencing any current difficulties, but I was on a roll and I was ready to rumble. With this prospect, because (say it with me) I'd done my homework, I knew to press the notion that I was willing and able to take any order from his company, even a small one, just to prove myself and my company to him. As luck would have it, this gentleman had a new item that would provide the perfect opportunity for me to pitch one of my products.

It was a chance for both of us to accomplish our respective goals. I wanted to prove my potential value to him, and he wanted to protect himself and his company by utilizing more than one supply source. We both walked away winners.

Driving back home I wondered, "What would have happened if I had simply turned around at the beginning of the day?" The answer was that I wouldn't have signed two new clients. The trip had been entirely worthwhile. I learned that day that I couldn't possibly know what might happen unless I made an effort, and that if I ever felt like I wanted to give up, take a pass, or do it another day, that other day may never come and someone else would come along and take my place. From then on, I knew that no matter how hard it might be some days, I had to remain disciplined, continue on, and never give up.

PART THREE

Human Effort Expanded

CHAPTER NINE

. . . .

Human Effort Expanded:
A Definition

Human effort is easy to understand in theory—we all have to put effort into almost everything we do each day—but what happens when you take that effort to its highest possible level? What would happen, for example, if you took the basics we went over in Parts One and Two, and gave them a creative boost that won't leave you gasping for air at the end of the day, but which will guarantee that you always leave the office knowing that you didn't stop at merely mediocre? Instead, you performed each and every step with intelligence, with gusto, and with pride. Wouldn't that make a real difference in your workday? Wouldn't that even give you a different perspective on life? Wouldn't that make it a little easier to get up every day feeling great about the work you do? And, in turn, wouldn't that make you a happier, more passionate, and ultimately a more successful human being?

I, for one, credit my success to adding everything I can to my personality, my presentation, and my follow-up. It doesn't require extra energy, or jumping around like a kangaroo in the office. It doesn't mean learning something new so much as taking what you already have and building upon it so that you leave clients and coworkers with an indelible impression of you as the person who will not only take business seriously, but who will take care of a client as if they were a member of the family. In this chapter, we'll talk about how you can achieve human effort expanded, and I'll share some tips with you about how you can make the absolute best impression on all the people you work with.

Human effort expanded does not translate to playing an unfamiliar role, nor does it ever include lying. Some people are born with natural charm and I say power to them! Others may think they have developed a certain persona, but they often come off as slick and disingenuous—an obvious red alert to any buyer or employer. Then, there are those of us who recognize certain talents we have—whether pointed out by another person or not—and we learn to build upon those talents, how to direct those talents, when to rein them in, and when to let them out full steam ahead.

I mentioned in Chapter One that I had an opportunity to host a radio show in the mid-1980s. I had always loved playing around with my voice; the kids at the orphanage had enjoyed my impressions and my silly range of characters. When I got in front of a microphone at the radio station, however, something in me was unleashed and I actually became known as "The Voice" amongst my friends and family. They took my newfound talent as something to giggle about, but I learned very quickly that this strong basso profundo, this simple change in the modulation of my voice that made me sound like a superhero of sales-people, brought in more clients than ever. Such a simple effort on my part made a huge difference in my success. Why? I'd thought outside of the box. I'd added a new trick to my salesman's repertoire of talents—simple, but amazingly effective.

Think about all the talents you have (for we all have many), and play around with what you can do to make a difference—to separate yourself from the rest of the competition. Make an assessment of everything from your customary greeting to your mannerisms, from the tone and speed of your speech to the way you make your exit. I believe one excellent way to begin is to try speaking to prospects and clients as if they are family, whenever appropriate.

When I talk to a prospect, customer, designer, or a line person at a company, I speak to them as if they are a part of my inner circle, as if I treasure their business, their expertise—as if I would rather be talking to them than anyone else in the world. When a meeting is over, sometimes the only appropriate way to end is to shake hands and extend thanks, along with a reminder that I'll always be there to answer any questions. I have also been known to give a client or a colleague a big hug too, though. It isn't intended to be disrespectful—heaven forbid—rather, it's a true show of sincerity and appreciation for someone going the extra mile for me. If a co-worker on the production line finds a way to improve the product, there's cause for a hug! With clients, it's very important to remember, however, that there's a time and place for making some kinds of physical contact, and you must always understand the limitations and boundaries of any person and every situation. Since you've done your homework (meaning you've collected all the information you can get your hands on) and you've observed your client's behavior closely, you'll know how to express your feelings under a variety of circumstances.

Why in the world am I talking about hugs in a sales book, you might ask? Because it's an example of human effort expanded. It's the things you do because you want to demonstrate that you truly appreciate it when someone helps you out; it's remembering the little things. Human effort expanded is exactly what it sounds like: going the extra distance without being pushy; acting with polished courtesy; exuding friendship and the willingness to help out whenever needed. It's going the extra mile because you realize how much that can be worth—both for your client or coworker and yourself. Is it always as simple as using a dynamic voice? Well, that depends on what you consider your talents to be. I found mine almost by mistake, but you may have to build your confidence before you can start experimenting with what your key will be to leaving them wanting more.

This final section of the book is mainly about that quickly fading practice of polite behavior and conversation with a twist, of making a business transaction something exciting and hopefully educational rather than just another day at the office shuffling papers and surfing the Net. It's about going the distance. Why? That's simple—because it's the right thing to do. I'll add here that I'm pretty disappointed these days by the general downfall of common courtesy. I was brought up to respect others, and to treat those who take time to help me especially well. I thank my family for my appreciation of respect, tact, sympathy, and empathy (and I can still smell the lasagna!).

Communication is an art that's been practiced for hundreds of years and celebrated by great authors, great philosophers, great artists, and all of the other people throughout history who have learned the beauty and importance of relating information and emotion. The art of letter writing is nearly gone, but if you have ever read letters from the first part of the twentieth century and before, you've seen that it was an act taken very seriously by the writer. Words were chosen carefully, and the sharing of both sad and happy news was practically poetic, particularly when compared to today's e-mail or text messages. I believe we have entirely too many gadgets today that prevent (and even sabotage) the art of communicating, person to person, in a civilized way. By this, I mean that our real personalities disappear when we are hiding behind a screen—the relationships and transactions we take part in via electronics seem removed, unmemorable, dry, and without any real feeling. You must be a person when you are dealing with other people so that they remember you first as a real human being when making decisions.

At this point in time, everyone contacts clients by means of a cell phone, a Blackberry, e-mail, text messaging, or any of the ever-growing market of devices that facilitate the sharing of information, but that also somehow interfere with a personal relationship with your prospects, clients, vendors, or colleagues. The problem (though I use the word "problem" reluctantly because there are some pretty amazing gadgets out there) is that we are humans, not robots. Whenever you communicate electronically, always follow up with a live call; let the person know that you, a living, breathing, caring human, will be available to them at any time, anywhere. It will take you just a few minutes to demonstrate that you're the salesperson they really can count on. Anyone over the age of 25 or 30 remembers those days when we actually got to know each other instead of trading pixels.

We have lost so much of the human element with advances in electronic communication, I sometimes find it more tragic than useful. Someone may be able to write the most eloquent and meaningful letter, but it must come from a real person, not generated by a machine. We—all of us—are inundated with information and tempted away from our work all day long, mostly from these gadgets and devices that are meant to make our lives easier. We can check sports scores, the latest stock market numbers; we can buy movie tickets, we can watch TV, we can play games, we can "chat" with people over the Internet, though it's mainly with strangers. (I'm still trying to figure out the social mechanics of meeting friends through telephone lines and satellites when there are real people—in the flesh—all around with whom one could socialize.)

Call me old-fashioned, but I want to offer you some sure-fire hints adopted from the good old days when people really did treat each other as fellow humans. They greeted each other with a bit more formality than we do these days, and then worked together toward establishing a personal relationship. Face-to-face meetings and voice-to-voice telephone calls whenever possible will absolutely put you in a better light than a garbled text message sent by Salesperson #2 while she is catching up on showbiz gossip and downloading her favorite song on the fascinating, colorful, eye-catching, never-let-you-go electronic box.

What you do off-hours is up to you, but I'd sure like to know how many hours are lost to Internet surfing, music downloading, and video games in one business day. These activities take no talent or effort; they swallow the time you need to find leads, to make follow up calls, to make sure the production line is clear on a recent change order, or even to spend time with your family. Sure, tell me it's a new world now, but I'd rather spend my time hunting down new prospects, taking a tour of a client's premises, learning all I can about my prospects and clients (using index cards, though I'll give in to using a Blackberry at this point) to store information about my clients, and most of all, sharing a laugh—in person—with a client. You can't really send a smile or a laugh via satellite. Again, this is an example of human effort expanded. Put yourself out there—smile, ask how you can help, share a joke with a lineman, send a Happy Birthday note to a buyer. Do whatever you can to stand out as the salesperson who doesn't simply act on request, but who goes in search of answers without being asked, who actively represents both your client and your company, always keeping everyone's best interests in mind.

Coming across as an authentic, on-the-ball, caring individual is your first step toward human effort expanded, and it will never fail you—you will always leave a positive impression. It's also important, though, to find something about yourself that you can use to cause a client or prospect to think, "Wow! What an interesting/creative/talented/ engaging/great guy/gal!" The "voice" was an obvious choice for me. Yours can also be centered around the way you speak—and you should absolutely practice this—or it may be a very impressive knowledge of how your client's business works. This is another example of human effort expanded I wholeheartedly believe in. It could be a certain way you've created to close a deal, or how you show your materials, or the enthusiasm in your eyes. Just make sure that you always maintain your integrity—never promise what you can't give and always avoid the stereotypical pushy salesman's rap. All of the suggestions above take a little extra effort than most salespeople are willing to give. I worked my way up the ladder at H.S. Crocker from salesman to CEO because I put in that little extra time for research, because I treated my clients and colleagues like real human beings, because I took the extra time to look at labels at the supermarket. Did I miss a few football games? Yup. Did I get frustrated sometimes? Absolutely. Do I regret so little free time? No way. The effort I spent has paid off very, very well. I am delighted with my career and that's something to take pride in.

CHAPTER TEN

The Rebirth of Compassion

Everyone has a God-given talent; blue-collar workers in manufacturing plants often have very specific talents they must use in order to produce or craft their piece of the finished product, but especially so that they can be proud of what they have created. In sales, your talent emerges as human effort, and your success may well rise and fall on the way your humanity shines through.

If you think this sounds odd, think of it this way: When you look in the mirror, do you see a compassionate person, or do you see someone who is only interested in making as much money for themselves as possible—damn everyone else involved! If the latter image is who you see, then perhaps you should reconsider your life strategy. Being a compassionate person means having the ability to understand others, and in doing so, you understand that you reap what you sow. Work hard, have fun, and above all, be a human being: kind, considerate, fair, honest, decent to others, and someone willing to put forth that little extra human effort. Not only that, but you ought to display respect for the job everyone else needs to perform to fulfill what you promised to your client. Respect is a two-way street—that's a prime ingredient for success in your career.

We sometimes become so caught up in our day-to-day activities that we lose sight of a basic fundamental of life: how we treat others, and how we respond to their positive or negative actions. In your earliest school days, you were taught patience, concentration, and when to be quiet. In sales, you will be exposed to every conceivable possibility when dealing with others, and you will find yourself calling upon those earlier lessons. How we adapt to and handle situations is the difference between being a great salesperson and merely an average salesperson.

Always remember to consider what your customers and prospects may be going through in their jobs and their lives. Never let a situation pass by that calls for a caring word, a get well card, or a thank you note (handwritten, not via e-mail). I remember a buyer I worked with who had recently lost his father. I called and offered my condolences and asked if there was anything I could do. His response was that I was the only salesperson on the vendor side that had expressed a true sense of loss and sympathy. He added that there was nothing I could do because simply making the phone call and offering my help was more than anyone else had done. Make no mistake—this type of gesture is part of superior sales skills. Showing empathy, understanding people's feelings, and offering what you can to help will guarantee that you aren't forgotten. I'm afraid that some of our younger salespeople neglect to show that they actually care about anyone but themselves. In my opinion, the goal is not just to get the order—it's to sell myself as well by ensuring my clients that they are working with someone who they truly can count on, someone who really does care.

Naturally, when you show kindness and consideration, it will set you apart and demonstrate that you are not only a salesperson representing your company, but you are also aware of how you represent yourself. In other words, you are someone with integrity. When you make a deal because your client recognizes those character traits in you, you'll know just how much your personal qualities have made a difference. Believe it: anyone will be more likely to buy from your company if you can cultivate that special trust, even if your competitor's product meets their needs better, and even if your competitor's prices are lower.

Keeping Cool under Difficult Circumstances

Another component of finesse, politesse, and human effort expanded is not losing your cool under difficult circumstances. Humor is a much better way to go. I've traveled with what seems like hundreds of people, many of whom have become ill-humored and visibly upset when things don't go their way. Some folks just can't control their emotions, but if I can ever turn a bad situation into one we can all get through without anyone losing their temper, I've won the day.

Several years ago, I had set up a national sales meeting to be held in Philadelphia on Thursday, September 12th. All of the attendees would be traveling from around the country on September 11th and would meet on the 12th, returning home on the 13th. My CFO, John Dai, my R&D director, and I all boarded a United flight, departing O'Hare at 8:00 a.m. The trip was uneventful until we were about halfway to Philly. That's when the pilot announced that we were having mechanical difficulties and we would be landing in Pittsburgh. By that time, we had no clue of what the rest of the world already knew. I remember thinking it was odd, as we rolled up the tarmac, because there were other planes parked and lined up all over the place. Yet when we deplaned and entered the terminal, there wasn't a soul around except for a corner bar that was just about to close. I looked around and saw that all the other shops were already closed. Finally, we came across a TV monitor where we learned what had happened at the World Trade Center and the Pentagon. In shock, we walked through the terminal to reach the tram that led to the main terminal, where a TV crew stopped to ask us where we were from. They did a short interview with me (my colleagues were very much shaken up, but I don't know if I've ever been at a loss for words) and then we continued on to the tram.

When we reached the main terminal there were no cars, buses, or rentals—not even a cab. I called our travel agent and she found a motel about ten miles away. We waited for a cab for over an hour. Finally, we got to the motel, but we were, for all intents and purposes, stranded without food, coffee, or even a bottle of water. That day was surreal and so very tragic for the victims, their families, and for so many people around the world. In a daze, my colleagues and I kept asking each other, Why? How could such a horrible thing happen? I certainly would never dream of making light of a tragedy so brutal, so unfair, so horrible, but the human effort I'd been practicing for so long kicked in immediately. I didn't want to cry, I wanted to comfort; I didn't want to sit, starving, staring at the terrifying images on TV, I wanted to attack the small problems we had immediately before us. There would be plenty of time for tears in the days and years to come.

We asked the motel manager to take us to a store where we bought hot dogs and hamburgers, beer and wine. She was especially glad that we were able to fix her outdoor gas grill so we could barbeque. She was friendly and helpful throughout our stay, which was so comforting on a day that had started off so miserably for so many—misery and fear we could all feel though we hadn't lost anyone ourselves. I felt like I needed to find some meaning in the devastation, but I simply couldn't until my friends and I were safely at home. We stayed that evening and all of the following day trying to get out with no luck; more frustrating still, no one seemed to have any answers.

On the second day, we learned about a train called the Midnight Special that was headed to Chicago. There were only three tickets left. I booked them, even though they couldn't guarantee there would be any extra food or provisions. We went to the downtown station by cab and when we boarded I noticed immediately that there were no guards and no security; we just showed our ticket and boarded. This, I felt, to say the least, was a reflection of what had gone wrong in the first place. Just two days after a major attack on our country, we had no protection whatsoever. Without sounding sarcastic, the country's security system was absolutely NOT showing effort expanded, nor had we run into much empathy from anyone, save our new friend at the motel. Instead of joining together to commiserate, or exchange information, or simply to be together as Americans on arguably the worst day in our country's history, people walked with eyes downcast, seemingly not ready or able to connect with their feelings or the feelings of a badly broken nation. It made me so sad—again, I wanted to comfort, not cry. I wanted to yell to everyone that everything would be okay, but of course I didn't.

The last time I'd been on a train was when I'd first joined the Army and I was on my way to basic training. The Midnight Special made several stops on the way to Chicago and whenever we slowed down, we'd ask what was going on. The delay was evidently due to a "bad track" or to wait for a freight train, as they have the right of way. We finally arrived in Chicago four days after we'd left. Despite everything we'd been through, and the general horror of what had happened to our country, it was a triumphant moment when we disembarked. For us, everything was okay. One of my salesmen picked us up in downtown Chicago and we went over to O'Hare to get my car, which was in the parking lot. Unfortunately, but probably appropriately, we could not travel into the airport area by car, so I took to my feet and walked a very long distance to the parking garage. Once we stopped at the office, looking like refugees, to check in, we all went home to anxious families who didn't care how we looked, just as long as we were home.

On a much lighter note, humor can turn a humdrum trip into something much more entertaining. On one summer day when I was still just a member of the sales team at Crocker, I was traveling to a small town in Kansas to see a prospective customer. I had been to see this prospect at least three or four times and since I knew I was getting close, I asked my manager to come along. I figured that if I brought along someone with a title, my pitch would be all the more impressive, and if there were any final decisions to be made, he would be there to bless them. It was a small town with a small terminal—the same person who rented cars out also took flight tickets and loaded the luggage on the plane.

On this particular trip, the airport attendant asked why we were in town. I replied, almost without thinking, that we were there to inspect the runway for cracks. I think the devil made me do it, but my boss, who enjoys humor as much as I do, went right along with it. The next day when we returned the car, the same airport employee was there and asked how it went. "I didn't see you our there inspecting the runway," she said. My boss, Al Trice, playing along, replied, "Oh, no. We were out there at four o'clock this morning." She asked again how it had gone, with a puzzled expression. Al replied, "Well, we found some cracks." She looked at me, now a bit alarmed, and asked, "What now?" I replied that we would have to come back with a caulking gun. Al and I looked at each other and began to laugh, then told her the real story. I still don't have any idea why we did it except that it was an amusing way to break up a long trip—just two pranksters trying to entertain ourselves in a town as big as a postage stamp. All I know is that if I lacked a sense of humor, I surely wouldn't have lasted in sales.

Folks have commented to me that I am very lucky to have the opportunity to travel so much. Well, yes and no, as you have read. Seeing new cities and flying all around the country seems glamorous at first, but the glimmer rubs off fairly quickly. The challenges require patience, knowing how to fill the time you'll spend waiting after your flight is cancelled and there's no hotel space, and most of all, humor. Catching a 5:00 a.m. flight and returning home at 9:00 p.m. is a hell of a long day, which can bring the worst out of anyone. What else can I say—it's part of the job.

Instead of feeding off the aggravation and losing your spirit and confidence, you need to cool down…and then fire up. Take a break for a meal or a drink, collect yourself, and then start working the phone, or answer your e-mails. There's always something to catch up on or to organize. Concentrate on work and you'll find the wait seems shorter. Take a look at the guy at the ticket counter about to pop a gasket because his vacation is being delayed for an hour or two and thank goodness you know how to accept what the world of travel dishes out. Whether it's a rough flight, a lost hotel reservation, or a national tragedy, stay alert, keep your emotions in check, rely on your sense of humor (again, if appropriate), and speak kindly to those who are having an even rougher time than you. If you're waiting in a crowd of people standing around, strike up a few conversations—you never know what will happen.

I always tell my salesmen, "Remember, if you get caught in a storm or a layover, your underwear is front to back, back to front, turned inside out, and again front to back and back to front. That's four days worth in all!" The moral is: expect the unexpected, stay cool as a cucumber, and never lose sight of the fact that we are all human beings who deserve respect. When you demonstrate that you are willing to speak to others with respect, wherever you are, they will almost always return the favor, and you may well have some memorable conversations.

I was in flight, returning from Denver recently, and I was seated next to a retired gentleman by the name of Harry. It was a very crowded airplane—I was in the middle seat and Harry was on the aisle. I've always taken special care to engage older folks in conversation. They are too often ignored, even though they are literally fonts of information and especially worthy of listening to. Even while seated, I could tell that Harry was a small man, perhaps standing at no more than five feet, and was probably well into his eighties. Well, here was Harry, minding his own business, when the cabin attendant bumped his elbow as she pushed the beverage cart down the aisle. Immediately, in a joking fashion, I said, "Harry, that's a workers comp claim, don't you think?" Harry looked up at me, eyes brightened by excitement, and when the attendant passed by again, he nudged me in the ribs and said to her, "This is my attorney and he thinks I have an elbow claim!" She laughed and said she was, in fact, dating a lawyer. I whispered to Harry that she must be crazy what with common opinion about lawyers.

As the trip progressed, Harry began to tell me about his life. I could literally feel how happy he was to chat with someone—he was radiant. He'd married at the age of 20 and had lived happily with his wife for 55 years. Sadly, his lifelong companion had passed ten years back and so he spent his time finding interesting things to do and see—a guy after my own heart. He explained that he lived in a retirement center, or an "institute," as Harry called it, a decision he'd made so that he wouldn't worry his children. He didn't want to make them fret over who would need to "take" him, or to care for him. He'd sold his house to one of his daughters with the understanding that on weekends—as his own wife and he had done—she would allow his handicapped son, who lived in a special home, stay with her on weekends. To his great relief, she had agreed and had kept her word. It was so important to Harry that his son experience the joy of family company and some of the beauty of the "outside world." It reminded me of the orphanage and the children I'd loved so much as a young man. Even more significantly, he was able to see his son, too, and he was able to do something for his child while he could still enjoy it.

Harry really got a kick out of having an eager listener; we talked for over two hours. At one point, he asked me what I did and what my title was. I replied that I was in printing and that my title was President/CEO. His eyes twinkled and he gave me a broad smile. "Oh my! I've never sat next to a President before!" When the plane landed, Harry leaned over close to me and said, "I've had so much fun on this trip, I can't believe it. Just wait until I tell the guys at the Institute!" As we exited the plane and walked toward the baggage claim, Harry thanked me over and over again for the conversation. I helped him find his way and then we parted with a hug and all the best wishes in the world. As I went my own way, I truly felt like an angel had looked down at me and had decided to let some of the little mistakes I'd made slide because I'd opened my heart to good ol' Harry—a true gentleman. All the way home in the car I had a lump in my throat, but a smile on my face.

You don't always have to be in "sales" mode to chat someone up. For me, it's often a matter of simply trying to brighten someone's day. I don't need to be selling something to offer a compliment, or to help a tourist with directions, or to strike up a conversation with someone who looks lonely. You have no idea how much happiness you can spread if you simply take the time to do it. I'm not sure of the rules of karma, but I do know that no good deed goes unnoticed (NOT unpunished), and sometime in the future you may find that someone—right out of the blue—will do something nice for you.

The Beauty of the Challenge

There's not a day that passes when I'm not enthusiastically waiting for the next challenge. That may be why so many businessmen enjoy golf—myself included—there's a similarity between the game and the life of a salesperson as I see it. There are plenty of clients you really need to put the energy boost pack on to work with, but then there are those that make it all worthwhile. Now, as a golfer I may play a great hole—either par or a birdie, and then I'll get good and fired up for the next hole. On the next hole I'll double bogie and feel like kicking myself. I'd never even consider quitting, though, at that point! I continue on to the next hole with the anticipation that I'll do better eventually, especially if I practice, and I play through the full 18.

Your challenges will be much the same in sales: you'll have a great day, and then the next day you'll be pounding your forehead on your desk. I can only advise that you consider that metaphor about the golf game; hell, apply it to any sport or hobby. We don't give them up out of frustration because we feel confident that they will bring us joy again in the future. Look forward to what the next day will bring, and leave yesterday behind you. Any time you bring excess baggage along with you into tomorrow, it will only pull you down. Move on!

I remember working on an account in Salina, Kansas, called Tony's Pizza. Their products are still in frozen food cases in supermarkets as I write. When I first saw their label on one of my countless trips to the supermarket (whether poor Darla was accompanying me or not, I don't recall), I noticed that Tony's Pizza was owned by Schwann's, the door-to-door food and ice-cream company, which is huge in the Midwest. I immediately called on Schwann's in Marshall, Minnesota, and I learned that I would have to work with a buyer in Salina and win him over before I could go any further. So, I began calling this gentleman on a persistent basis. Finally, after three months, I convinced him that it was worth his time to meet with me. Unfortunately, when I met him for the very first time, I found out that he was in love with his Wichita supplier. Oh, blasted romance!

After several months of staying the course (because a great salesperson never gives up!), I finally convinced him that we should try a test run. I explained—because I'd absolutely done my homework, down to who was romancing whom—that my company could be a second source of supply for handling the low-volume short runs. Plus, a backup supplier would surely make sense. At that point, it had taken me one full year of follow-up just to reach that point!

As I recounted earlier in the "Trip From Hell," numerous problems occurred with this particular test run: ingredients on my company's labels were transposed, halting production; our Baltimore plant had sold the machine that put the grease-resistant coating on the back of the labels, and the alternative solutions were more costly; and then there were those mishaps on the twin-engine flight. Was I disappointed by some of those events? Sure, but that doesn't mean I ever gave up. More importantly, while working on this prospect, I was still cultivating other business possibilities so that if this one fell through, I had the others. Does a salesperson want all possibilities to come through? Of course, but that rarely happens in the real world. That is why you must always have other projects in development and why you must always be ready to face the next challenge so that setbacks do not become major obstacles in your sales growth.

A truly successful salesperson doesn't just hope everything will work out. Instead, he or she looks for challenges, and to top it off, they actually enjoy challenges. There's nothing to fear. If you can find beauty in a challenge, you will find that it works like the domino effect. Solve one major challenge and you'll want to do it again, only better still than the last. It's what life is all about, in a way. We all face challenges every day; it's how we handle them that makes the difference.

Making Time for Both Family and Career

Anyone who works full-time and has a family knows how challenging it can be to maintain both to the best of your ability. Human effort expanded can also be applied to family life, however. It's not easy to build an ace salesperson's account base and still have time left over for a meaningful relationship with your family, especially if you have children and there are baseball games and ballet recitals to attend. To balance your family life and career successfully, you and your significant other need to work together as a team; your partner needs to understand what your goals are, and what your success will bring to the entire family. Is it easy? No, of course not, but then again, life in general isn't always easy. Whatever we do in life demands sacrifice and patience, but that doesn't necessarily mean your family comes second. My own father worked endless hours and we didn't have a lot of time with him, but he was always at the dining room table for dinner and he always made time to talk if we needed him.

Earlier in my career, during the weekdays, I worked long hours, both at the office and with customers and prospects. On the weekends, there were many phone calls I needed to make and there were some Saturdays I had to go into the office, but I always made time to coach my daughter's baseball team or my son's karate class and attend their tournaments. Was it a juggling act? Yes, in fact it was the same juggling act my wife had to do every day of the week with the kids. Communication and planning ahead so there aren't too many surprises is key. Remembering to "be in the moment" is also a must. When you're at the office, your mind should be whizzing and whirling with business ideas and projects; when you're at your daughter's ballet recital, it's so terribly important that your attention is focused on what your daughter has worked so hard on for you to see. Human effort expanded means that you must learn to make every day, every hour, and every minute count.

Have things gotten any less crazy the longer I've been in sales? Well, yes and no. Although it is easier now with the kids grown up, there are still times when my wife's patience wears thin. In the end, however, we have been able to live comfortably, help our children, and give charitably to those who so desperately need it. We are not swimming in cash, by any means, but we do believe in letting our children enjoy our gifts while we are still living rather than after we are gone.

You will encounter periods in your career and family life that will serve as character builders, even if it takes a while for you to recognize it. As CEO of H.S. Crocker, I have had times when I have not only had monumental work responsibility, but charitable work to attend to as well. And on top of that, family emergencies have complicated the situation even more on occasion. My wife experienced complications with eye surgery at the same time that I had to make an emergency trip to Florida to help my son with his storm-damaged home from Hurricane Francis. Yes, it was nearly maddening, but a few months later, I realized certain ways my character had been built from such adversity. I realized that I truly had expanded my effort and I felt proud and so grateful to have had the opportunity to prove it to myself, my colleagues, and, of course, to my family.

On another occasion, quite a few years before my wife's eye surgery, my wife and children experienced another tragedy, which helped us all to build our characters even though we didn't realize it at first. Just a few days before his ninth birthday, our son was hit by a car on the way home from his karate class, which he loved. Our brick bungalow—a popular style in and around Chicago—was on a residential corner. I was working in the living room when I heard a screech and then a thump. I looked out the window and there was my son, lying like a rag doll in the street. After many weeks in the hospital, we still had to ride home in an ambulance—the poor kid was in a full body cast and had to be maneuvered sideways through the front door. His younger sister referred to him simply as "boy," as if she didn't realize the child in the body cast was, in fact, her brother. For quite a long while afterward, our lives became almost impossibly complicated but we managed because that's what human effort expanded allows you to do.

We all had heavy hearts during this time, but somehow we found a way, and I became even more determined to assure my family that I would take care of them, emotionally and financially, as long as I lived. As the saying goes, what doesn't kill you only makes you stronger. At the same time, I decided that it was more important than ever to help others, because that's what makes life truly satisfying in a non-selfish way. To touch a stranger's life is to share a miracle, leaving you to believe that miracles happen to all sorts of people every day. It's not an occasion to feel like a hero, or a saint, or anything but yourself—someone who helped out a fellow human being when they most needed it. Like any family, we suffered: but we always kept in mind the very real fact that there are many people out there with problems worse than our own.

If you try to make the best of your talent and balance the needs of your family, there is always a way. As long as your partner is on board with what you're doing, you will find less turmoil in your life, and if you can teach your children, or even other salespeople at your office, the basics of human effort expanded, you will have made a real difference in the way your life progresses positively, right along with those you are willing to share with.

CHAPTER ELEVEN
· · · · · · · · · · · · · · · · · · · ·

Life in the Travel Lane

We've all had the pleasure of trains, planes, and whatnot—oh yes, can't forget buses—and the life experiences that are endured over the miles. I travel by plane mostly, so that will be the setting for this travel odyssey. Recall for a moment the excitement of air travel: coughs, colds, spills, barf, delays, cancellations, and lost crews. Will it ever end? Probably not! So get ready to take off your shoes and belt, empty your pockets, remove that coat, and get out those small bottles of liquids, because you're going through security. Stay to your right, and have your ID ready. Don't try to be funny, and don't start thinking your time is important. You're just another pretty face here. (At least I think you're pretty.)

Now you've passed through the metal detector. Ah, but wait a minute: they need to swab your bag while impatient travelers in line behind you close in. Half your clothes are off at this point, and your shoes and other belongings are in a basket you can't see. But the finish line is in sight. You can do it! Go for the gold! Just not yet.

Before you grab your stuff—remain calm and assume your most casually confident look as you wait for the results. Your baskets of clothing are arriving on the conveyer, recalling your school-cafeteria days, when you readied yourself to grab the best-looking piece of pie. You get the green light: it's time to gather your things and get out of the way. Heads up: you're about to be hit by a purse flung over a lady's shoulder coming up fast on the inside lane. Close call. Don't stop now. Grab those trays full of your stuff, stand your ground, dress as fast as you can, and move over to the far lane. Phew, safe.

Relieved to make it through the stress of the security checkpoint? Don't get ahead of yourself; you haven't even boarded. More adventures are coming. You're flying stand-by, which should teach you a vital lesson: don't change your flight at the last minute or try to get an earlier flight. It will only earn you the rare and distinguished privilege of a middle seat. Life in the middle seat is reserved for an elite group that has learned how to pin their elbows to their ribs, sit still, avoid breathing deeply, and keep that guy next to them from falling asleep and using their shoulder for a pillow.

Now you're in the air, well into the first hour of a two-hour flight. Uh-oh, you need to use the restroom. Not good: you may be perceived as a troublesome seat companion, and you'll more than likely cede any sacred space you've earned through your determination and willingness to stand your ground. But the real test of your mettle comes when you're seated in the middle seat in the last row, just in front of the bathrooms. Bet you thought, how could it get any worse? Well, your answer comes in the form of two six-footers arriving to flank you in the aisle and window seats. No reclining human walls on either side of you, the regular whoosh of lavatory flushes, a line of people lurking in the aisle as they wait to relieve themselves, and last in line for that still-free soft drink. Drink fast, you were last to be served, but those trays need to be in the upright and locked position for landing.

Turns out the flight attendant is having a bad day. That's understandable; we all have them. But his curt tone hardly smooths the ragged tempers of your fellow flyers. Frozen wages, terrible hours, belligerent passengers to shepherd—what else could someone ask for in a career? Now you get to handle the crabby customer sitting next to you—lucky day. They say patience is a virtue, but I think it's a penance more than anything else. She doesn't want to put her tray up for you, and she insists on getting another drink before landing. Makes it very difficult to escape your cage to use the restroom. Oh boy, cross your legs and pray. You're sure it's a saving grace when the pilot comes over the speaker and announces: "Weweeeee blannnntha bfoflytempouts iiiiii———— deggggggggs." What the hell did he say? Modern technology has given so much to today's aircraft but in-flight announcements—well, even my rabbit-ear antennas have more clarity.

Still, it won't be long before we land. You're feeling better already. Feels like the plane is descending. Soon another announcement, this one less garbled: we'll need to circle for a few minutes. Keep the faith. We're getting serious about the landing approach now. Okay, we're finally on the ground, taxiing and taxiing—and, sigh, stopping in an area known as the penalty box. What did we do? It must be a mistake; we're good, honest people. Please don't punish us. We'll be good. We promise. You wait for your release restlessly. Low and behold, a miracle: the plane proceeds to the gate.

So now you're walking to catch the shuttle that will bring you to the rental car VIP lot so you can go see your customer—you know, the reason you made the trip at all. You arrive and glance at the VIP board to find your name and space number for the car that should be ready and waiting. (That's what VIP service can do for you, they promise.) Your name's not there, so you proceed to the counter to ask where you can find your reserved car. And, predictably, the reply is one of the following (as per the Book of Car Rentals, chapter ten, verse fifteen): 1) we didn't have a chance to put your name up there; 2) your flight was late, so we took your name off the board; or 3) we don't have a current credit card number on file. Well, let's see, you entered your new expiration date on the rental company's website, so that should have eliminated number 3. As for number 2, why would your name be removed if you've neither picked up your car nor canceled it? And accounting for number 1— they didn't have a chance to put your name up—let's just blame the computer. You knew you should have traveled on Tuesday instead of Wednesday.

At last you drive off in your super-deluxe minivan (boy, your colleagues back at the office would be proud; you reserved a midsize but, who knows, maybe your customer will need you to haul a little league team?). You arrive at your customer's office, conduct your business, and head back to the airport—to return the car, go through security, etc., etc. This time you're treated to the pleasure of the body scanner. You and the rest of the herd stand docile listening to the TSA agents: Take everything out of your pockets! No belts, no change, no wallets, no keys! Thank God we're keeping our pants on. Now the big decision: Where do you put your wallet? You notice that some stash it in their shoe, others in their coat pocket, but you prefer your briefcase.

You pass the scan and proceed to your gate only to see the sinkingly familiar announcement on the board—DELAYED. "For how long?" you ask the agent at the desk.

"We don't know, but we'll keep you advised. As soon as we know, we'll make an announcement." That is such a loving, kind, and gentle response you want to hug the agent right there on the spot. (Could happen.)

So it's time for phone calls, e-mail, and a bite to eat, knowing full well that you're either here for the duration and should book a hotel room or will likely be on the midnight shuttle. The next announcement, offered at 11:00 a.m., shares the reassuring news that two mechanics are working on the problem, so it shouldn't take a long time. You keep telling yourself to stay hopeful. But then you look out the gate window and see one mechanic staring at the engine and the other holding bolts in his hand with an expression that telegraphs "I wonder where these go?"

Soon it's 2:00 p.m. and another announcement comes along: "Well, folks, we're going to borrow some parts from our neighbors at Blank Blank Airlines because we don't have repair parts at this airport. But don't worry, we'll get you going soon!" Yeah, you've heard that before.

You enter your second phase of advanced waiting: finding a table at an airport restaurant for lunch. You get to know the waitress, the folks on either side of your small table, and the bookstore salesperson. When you return to the gate, you hear another announcement. They're flying in a part from Chicago. It will be here in two hours, and then they can finish the repair. That extends the whole process to 4:30 or 5:00 p.m. With any luck, we should be out of here by 8:00! People are getting restless; they begin lining up at the counter to switch to another carrier. Uh-oh, counter reinforcements. That's never a good sign. Two agents and a supervisor are on hand to calm the herd. After twenty minutes of back-and-forth, you get another late-breaking update: we'll depart in one hour, if all goes well.

Surprise. It doesn't go well, so you line up for your hotel and food certificates, which will barely cover a McDonald's meal and a hotel five miles from the airport. You decide to write down the plane's number just to see if you get the same plane the next day. Yes, the next morning you arrive and see that it's same plane but only half full because so many others made other arrangements or rebooked for another day. Finally, the repaired plane is landing at your home airport—what could be better? As John Denver once sang in one of his songs, "Hey, it's good to be back home again."

. . . .

Many of us who travel all the time encounter a number of challenging situations. Sharing a few representative anecdotes with those who haven't had as many travel adventures, well, that only seems fair. Here are just a few.

1.   Traveling from Dallas to Chicago on an 8:00 p.m. flight departure, I'm in the rear of a fairly empty aircraft in an aisle seat. The row behind me is empty, as are the rows in front and directly across the aisle. In the row diagonally across, is a couple. The flight attendant comes down the aisle, eyes wide open—and I mean really wide open—because the couple is having an intimate moment. She is sitting on her companion's lap, facing him, and . . . well, use your imagination. The silver lining is that at least it didn't last long. No staying power, I guess.

2.   Flying from Miami to Bermuda, I'm dressed nicely, wearing a sport coat I neatly fold and place on top of my bag in the overhead bin. The flight attendant stuffs a carry-on into the bin, crushing my jacket. "Excuse me, sir," I pipe up, "but you're crushing my jacket."

      He looks at me, apparently amazed that I would even worry about it. "Do you have a problem with making full use of the bin space?"

      "Not at all. I only object to my sport coat being crushed. Can you please refold it and place it on top?"

      "I'll get right back to you!" he said as he moved away.

He never did, so the folks across the aisle let me use their overhead. The takeaway from that experience is that overstuffing the bins is okay on certain trips, especially if the flight attendant is having a bad day.

3.   On a trip to Florida with my wife, just as we reach our cruising altitude, the flight attendant asks what we'd like to drink. It's early morning, so we choose two black coffees. We hit some rough air as the flight attendant is handing me my *hot, hot* coffee, and it spills on my jeans. Not so hot as to cause pain, just embarrassment for both of us. She comes running back with a dry towel and is about to dab at my jeans, at which point we look at each other and laugh. I don't think my wife, sitting right next to me, will approve of that move, since the coffee fell in my crotch. Yikes! We all laugh, acknowledging that we've just shared one of those unforgettable travel moments.

For a seasoned traveler, each trip-related misadventure takes on a special meaning. You begin to understand the scary truth that those somewhat nutty turns of events are what it's all about. Sometimes it's the God's honest truth that if you don't laugh you'll cry—so you might as well just get used to surfing the ups and downs of travel. The airlines and their employees are trying their best to keep us safe, and they work at being on time. But things happen, and we should remind ourselves to stay grateful that they take safety measures and procedures seriously. So you should take advantage of the inevitable waiting and frequent unexpected delays to get caught up and to contact your customers and prospects. If you do, it will be time well spent.

CHAPTER TWELVE

· ·

Final Thoughts

The paths we take in life can make wild twists and turns and most of the time we aren't quite sure where they will lead. Naturally, it's up to us to make sure a path is not a dead end. If you're working hard but making no headway, then you have to realize that you may be in the wrong field or with the wrong company. If you just sit back and collect a paycheck, it won't be long before dissatisfaction catches up with you. Yes, I have made changes during my career What is most important is to be able to recognize when a change is needed, and then to make a well-researched move. Will you always make precisely the right move? Of course not. If we were all that good, we wouldn't be on this earth, but in a higher realm. The important thing is to try, and someday you will find that special place that makes you want to work as hard as you possibly can—to expand your human effort to its fullest capacity.

If you are considering sales at a young age, try getting a part-time sales job first and see where it leads you. If you don't like what you are selling, or if you are uncomfortable with the people you must deal with on a daily basis, give it another shot with a different company—as in all fields, there are companies that are winners, and then there are the duds. If you feel that you are selling the wrong product, then find another sales job that interests you and give it another try. You'll soon find out whether or not sales is for you, because if it doesn't work on the second try—if you just don't jibe with the people you are working with, the people you are selling to, or the product you're meant to sell—then I would advise that sales may not be the right field for you. Just because you love to talk to people doesn't mean that you're a natural candidate for sales; it just means that you are an outgoing person. Sales is much more than simply chatting someone up—there is follow up, inconveniences, travel (sometimes with less than accommodating accommodations), and myriad other things you will be responsible for. Many people are outgoing, but they just can't handle the pressure of selling.

Also, when considering sales as a career, you owe it to yourself to consider whether it will interfere with other goals you have set for yourself. Sales doesn't leave a lot of free time to travel the world, to play guitar in a touring rock band, to raise a family of eight, or to sleep in. Sales is very demanding, so if you envision a slower-paced life with a lot of free time, then a different career choice is your best bet.

Personally, to this day, I still feel a rush when I work on a project and see it through its successful progression. I have not lost that love over the past thirty-five years; in fact, the more I do, the more I want to do. That's how your experience in sales should make you feel, too. There isn't a career on earth that will ensure that every day is a happy and fruitful one. But I guarantee that even if you just make a couple of contacts, or brainstorm about what you can do to close a deal, or practice your pitch in front of a mirror until you discover something new you can use, that will be a day well spent. In other words, if you do something each and every day to improve your sales technique and your personal charisma, you are on the road to success. Then, when you're at the office, you can spend your time getting the more concrete tasks done. You can do it. After all, if you really put your mind and energy to it, anything is possible.

That said, all of us grow up thinking about what we'll be, and later in life, how we'll end our careers. At the end of your career, you will have something no one can take away from you. That something is knowing in your heart and mind that all of the sales calls and all the travel has made you a better, more responsible, more knowledgeable person. You will have had the opportunity to meet countless people, and whether you found them pleasant or unpleasant, there is always something to be learned, even if you don't realize it right away. You have developed the talent to sell to people when others have failed. Is that a good feeling? No, it's a great feeling! Always remember: you have shared your beliefs and dreams of success with every prospect you have ever encountered, and every prospect who became a customer. This is something you will cherish for the rest of your life.

You believed, and you succeeded. Don't sell yourself short, don't lose sight, and stay focused.

In sales, you must be willing to give, and you must understand that even if you are in a better place than someone else, that doesn't make you any better than they are as a person. You are never superior and no one is beneath you. This is not a rule many people follow; it's easy to get caught up in competition mode with your competitors, or even with your fellow salespeople at the company you work for. I have met salespeople with all different sorts of personalities, some polite and respectful, some unnecessarily opinionated and bellicose. After having read this book, you know well where I stand on the issue of respect and politesse. With encouragement from my family, friends, and community, I realized the relative benefits of giving very early in life. Now I truly believe that what you do for others comes back tenfold. If your heart is full, it will serve as an anchor. No one can do something alone. You cannot be the star of your own show; you need supporting characters to guide you and open-minded people to sell to. So, my first most important lesson is never to lose your temper. In fact, it would do you well never to lose your charm, either. Treat every single person you come across with respect and always offer a smile. I cannot overemphasize how important it is, for example, to really bend over backwards for the guys behind the scenes: the linemen, the machinists, the support staff, and anyone else whose day might brighten a bit as a result of having not only been noticed but to have been appreciated.

As I mentioned before (surely more than once), it's absolutely crucial that you love your product. When I was a kid and I had fashioned my little hot dog stand, I certainly loved and stood behind my "product." Later, as a young man, when I turned a hole-in-the-wall beauty shop into a veritable "Beauty Garden," the same was true. But loving something and being proud of it doesn't mean never letting it go; in truth, the pride I felt when I sold those things—the fact that other people recognized the merit of my product—made me even happier than creating them in the first place.

You might ask, "How in the world can you develop love for a yogurt lid or a tire or some newfangled widget of some kind?" I'll answer that you can love and appreciate anything as long as you can find the merit in it. Your manager or boss should be able to tell you exactly why the product you have been hired to sell is the very best of its kind, why it's worthy of so much praise. Then you must become intimate with the product—touch it, look at all of its moving parts, test it out, know the product like you know the back of your hand. There simply is no way to be a successful salesperson if you don't care for whatever it is you are selling. People, especially buyers, have a sixth sense about these things. In fact, I'd bet that any buyer with some time under his belt will literally smell the fear if you aren't 100% behind your product, and you'll have lost the sale within minutes of entering the office. The buyer has the upper hand in a sales relationship—show him or her that you know your stuff frontwards, backwards, and sideways!

The third lesson from this book I'd like to reiterate is honesty. If, for example, you don't honestly care about your product, my advice would be to find a different company to work for rather than lie to a customer. Dishonest salespeople give all salespeople a shady reputation. While it sometimes isn't necessarily their fault, but rather the fault of a needless or deficient product, it's my opinion that a salesperson is flat out dishonest if he or she is overstating what a product can do. I wouldn't be able to live with myself if it meant lying to folks all day. I'd find it downright depressing. On the other hand, because I have always had unflagging faith in my product, no matter what it is, I walk proudly into any sales appointment. I enjoy a cup of yogurt now and then, and I sure would appreciate it if when I open the lid, the yogurt won't spill or spray down the front of my suit jacket. Is that a big deal? Well, yes. I dare say anyone would choose a compliant yogurt over an explosive one, no? There is something to love about anything useful, even though it might seem mundane. We need and use dozens of products daily, never thinking about why or how they work—that's your job as a salesperson.

Along with honesty, charity has always been a cornerstone of my own life plan. I'm sure it dates back to my wonderful experience with the orphanage and the children there. As a child, I never understood why I had been lucky enough to have a loving, close family, yet these beautiful, friendly children seemed to have been given so much hard luck. We all complain about things that seem to be monumental irritants until we remember those people who have much more difficult lives than we do. We all huff and puff over having to stop at the market for a forgotten item—a waste of ten minutes! But do we stop and remind ourselves about the victims of Hurricane Katrina, who had no food for days at a time? When we grumble about a head cold, do we remember those who have circumstances far worse than our own? It's often enough to make a soul feel guilty about simply being able to support a family, particularly in a busy and fast-paced city where selfishness often rules the day!

The answer is to commit yourself not only to giving what you can to those in need, but to perform random acts of kindness whenever possible. I am not to be commended for my reaction to 9/11, but I did try to console the people I was with, I never lost my cool, and I never once felt sorry for myself. For me, the days following were inconvenient, but not life-shattering. Charity to me means giving, yes, giving of yourself and helping others. When I chatted with my dear friend Harry on the airplane trip, he thanked me over and over, as if I had done him a favor. Quite the opposite. I found every moment of conversation as enjoyable as he did and I thank him for his wisdom and his charity toward me.

You've no doubt noticed that this book is not limited to sales technique alone. It has been terribly important to me to share another message as well. It's a simple message but it is also as profound as can be. While it's true that sales has never been known as a particularly charitable profession, it really does provide so many opportunities to spread some happiness. Charity is not limited to giving money or material objects—it can also consist of something as simple as a smile. Obviously, I'm no stand-up comic; I'm not a great orator, and I have no vast sums of cash to divvy out. I do like to think, though, that I really can brighten someone's day just by being friendly, by listening, by telling someone they're doing a good job. If you were given the choice between a job sitting behind a desk like a big dog, counting your money and barking orders, or taking a job where you can perform all the tasks at hand and you can promote and add to a successful work environment where people treat each other with kindness and honesty, which would you pick? Only you can answer that question.

Much of the joy I've found in creating this book has been in proving my theories on paper. Before I began, I wondered if I could clearly communicate this utopian mixture of a sales technique manual and a call to arms for everyone to reassess their own decisions and the way in which they perform their jobs—indeed, how they live their lives. As I named it in a previous chapter, I hoped that this would be a "sales book plus," that you the reader would take away much more than how to pitch a product, how to close a deal, and how to follow up correctly. I sincerely hope that a larger message comes through   one that encourages you to bring out the best in yourself, not simply so that you can be proud and make a good salary, but so that you, too, can experience the joy of giving.

The tips, tricks, and resources I've provided here are tried and true. I do guarantee that if you follow my methods, you can succeed as a salesperson. There's no room for failure if you are knowledgeable, en-thusiastic, and organized. The suggestions I've made concerning how you live your life and how you treat others don't necessarily come from my work experience, but they are things I've learned along the way that have made my work a joy rather than a chore. How you choose to apply your personality is entirely up to you, though I do hope you make some time for those less fortunate than you. In order to raise the char-acter of our country, we must be willing to take an active part. Mentor a student, give to your favorite charity, put some time in at your local elder care center, or spend an hour or two reading aloud to hospital patients. For every human, there is a cause, and for every cause, there is a needy human. I consider the charity work I do as necessary; I feel that the world has given me so many wonderful opportunities, it's only right to give back.

I hope I've spread a bit of wisdom; I hope I've encouraged some enthusiasm. I hope I've given you a few ideas about appearance, body language, pride for your product, and most importantly, pride in yourself because you know you'll stop at nothing to get the job done, honestly and expertly, from beginning to end. I hope most of all that I've given you some perspective as it relates to your fellow human beings, because there are few things you can do that will make you feel better.

I've also been realistic: some folks just don't take to the rigors of the job. Time spent trying to make a square peg fit into a round hole is time wasted. Those of you with the relative advantage of youth have more time to explore opportunities (as I did)—just be sure you don't get caught in a rut, staying with the same company out of convenience alone. But that's a nice thing about sales, too. It is not an "ageist" field. A person of almost any age has a good shot of making a new career for themselves if they work hard, apply themselves, and keep an open mind.

The ball is in your court now. Keep this book handy so that you can return to certain sections for advice or support. Studies have shown that you can direct your life's path simply by thinking of it—by imagining success and happiness rather than fearing the next hurdle and climbing under the proverbial rock. In other words, success is a choice, and it's your choice alone. Some people just seem to wake up with a smile on their face—I'm one of those lucky souls—and that's what I want for you.

THE END